"Breathtaking! *The Women of Christmas* is tender and joy filled and funny and faithful. With genuine warmth, profound wisdom, and refreshing wonder, Liz Curtis Higgs offers up a perfect seasonal blend—just what every woman in the midst of Christmas needs. I savored every word."

—ANN VOSKAMP, author of the *New York Times* bestseller *One Thousand Gifts: A Dare to Live Fully Right Where You Are*

"Liz Curtis Higgs ably mines the Scriptures, revealing undiscovered treasures in the familiar story. Through the pages of this powerful little book, we get to peer into the hearts of these women and find our own hearts melting at the beauty of God's grace."

—NANCY GUTHRIE, author of the Bible study series Seeing Jesus in the Old Testament

"This season delight your friends with an early gift of *The Women of Christmas,* inviting them to see how Elizabeth, Mary, and Anna were part of God's great plan to rescue us. As Liz puts it, 'Never doubt for a moment that women matter to the Almighty.'"

—DEE BRESTIN, author of *Idol Lies: Facing the Truth About Our Deepest Desires*

"*The Women of Christmas* invites us to steal away with our Savior during the hustle and bustle of one of the busiest seasons of the year. In her warm and welcoming voice, Liz Curtis Higgs draws us into the compelling stories of the women who surrounded our Messiah's birth and encourages us to consider our own relationship with him. An inspirational and biblically rich devotional. What a wonderful way to experience Christmas!"

—KELLY MINTER, author of *Nehemiah: A Heart That Can Break*

The
Women
of
Christmas

OTHER BOOKS BY LIZ CURTIS HIGGS

NONFICTION
Bad Girls of the Bible
Really Bad Girls of the Bible
Unveiling Mary Magdalene
Slightly Bad Girls of the Bible
Rise and Shine
Embrace Grace
My Heart's in the Lowlands
The Girl's Still Got It

CONTEMPORARY FICTION
Mixed Signals
Bookends

HISTORICAL FICTION
Thorn in My Heart
Fair Is the Rose
Whence Came a Prince
Grace in Thine Eyes
Here Burns My Candle
Mine Is the Night
A Wreath of Snow

CHILDREN'S
The Parable of the Lily
The Sunflower Parable
The Pumpkin Patch Parable
The Pine Tree Parable
Go Away, Dark Night

LIZ CURTIS HIGGS

Best-selling author of *The Girl's Still Got It*

The Women *of* Christmas

Experience the Season Afresh with

ELIZABETH, MARY, *and* ANNA

WATERBROOK
PRESS

THE WOMEN OF CHRISTMAS
PUBLISHED BY WATERBROOK PRESS
12265 Oracle Boulevard, Suite 200
Colorado Springs, Colorado 80921

All Scripture quotations, unless otherwise indicated, are taken from the Holy Bible, New International Version®, NIV®. Copyright © 1973, 1978, 1984, 2011 by Biblica Inc.™ Used by permission of Zondervan. All rights reserved worldwide. www.zondervan.com. For a list of the additional Bible versions that are quoted, see pages 209–10.

Hardcover ISBN 978-1-60142-541-6
eBook ISBN 978-1-60142-542-3

Cover design by Kelly L. Howard

Published in the United States by WaterBrook Multnomah, an imprint of the Crown Publishing Group, a division of Penguin Random House LLC, New York.

WATERBROOK and its deer colophon are registered trademarks of Penguin Random House LLC.

Library of Congress Cataloging-in-Publication Data
Higgs, Liz Curtis.
    The women of Christmas : experience the season afresh with Elizabeth, Mary, and Anna / Liz Curtis Higgs. — First Edition.
        pages cm
    Includes bibliographical references.
    ISBN 978-1-60142-541-6 — ISBN 978-1-60142-542-3 1. Jesus Christ—Nativity.
2. Christmas. 3. Mary, Blessed Virgin, Saint. 4. Elizabeth (Mother of John the Baptist), Saint. 5. Anna (Biblical prophetess) 6. Bible. Luke I–II—Criticism, interpretation, etc.
I. Title.
    BT315.3.H53 2013
    232.92—dc23

                                                    2013024706

Printed in the United States of America
2016

15 14 13

SPECIAL SALES
Most WaterBrook Multnomah books are available at special quantity discounts when purchased in bulk by corporations, organizations, and special-interest groups. Custom imprinting or excerpting can also be done to fit special needs. For information, please e-mail SpecialMarkets@WaterBrookMultnomah.com or call 1-800-603-7051.

To my sister-in-law,
Annie,
born on Christmas Day.

You are a gift to our family
and to everyone who knows you.
Bless you for encouraging me
in so many ways, dearie,
year after year.
I love you.

Contents

One   Let Every Heart Prepare
Him Room 1

Two   Let All Mortal Flesh Keep Silence . . . 21

Three   The Virgin Mother Kind 37

Four   O Tidings of Comfort and Joy . . . 59

Five   With Heart and Soul and Voice . . . 83

Six   The Wondrous Gift Is Given 113

Seven   And Our Eyes at Last Shall
See Him 139

Eight   Joy of Every Longing Heart 165

Study Guide 181

Notes 195

Heartfelt Thanks 211

One

Joy to the world, the Lord is come!
Let earth receive her King;
Let every heart prepare him room,
And heaven and nature sing,
And heaven and nature sing,
And heaven, and heaven, and nature sing.

—ISAAC WATTS, "JOY TO THE WORLD," 1719

Let Every Heart
Prepare Him Room

*L*ong before silver bells jingled, Christmas lights twinkled, and horse-drawn sleighs went dashing through the snow, God reached down from heaven with the best gift of all.

Love, wrapped in swaddling clothes.

Hope, nestled in a manger.

Three women played vital roles in the Messiah's birth: Elizabeth, Mary, and Anna. Even if you've met them before, I think you'll enjoy getting to know them better. And I'll love sharing the journey with you!

Their lives were markedly different. Elizabeth was married, settled, mature. Her kinswoman Mary was young, still living at home, and engaged to a carpenter. Anna was an elderly widow whose every waking hour was wholly dedicated to God. Before we reach the final page, we'll understand why God chose them.

And why—this part boggles my mind—God has chosen us too.

We'll also spend time with the men in their lives, including an old priest called Zechariah, a new husband named Joseph, and a brother of the faith known as Simeon.

Still, it's the women who carry the story, teaching us by example to wait upon the Lord, to trust him with everything that matters to us, to pray until our prayers are answered. We'll also hear from more than two dozen women who shared their comments through my online Bible study. Their honesty and humility bring these ancient stories right into the present, showing us what it means to surrender our lives to the One who loves us most.

And he truly does love you. Always has, always will. If only one message from this book finds a home in your heart, let it be that God's love for you is wider, longer, higher, and deeper than you can ever imagine!

Christmas is so much more than a holiday. So much more than buying and wrapping and cooking and eating and trimming with tinsel and mailing out cards. It's a season for reflection, for preparation, for renewal. The perfect time to put aside our shopping lists and reach for our Bibles, where the story of the Christ child awaits us.

Curl up in a comfy spot, and let's dive in.

"This year I want to look up and be refreshed anew by the true meaning of it all."

—MIRIAM

And so we begin with Elizabeth, our first woman of Christmas.

Anticipation builds as we turn to the book of Luke. We know what's coming. Or do we? The forgotten details, the overlooked truths may catch us by surprise and teach us something new about God and his love for us. The birth of his Son is a story that never grows old, never loses its power to alter our thinking and realign our priorities.

Mary is, of course, the most famous of our trio, yet her older kinswoman Elizabeth moved into the limelight first, along with the man she married.

> In the time of Herod king of Judea there was a priest named Zechariah,... *Luke 1:5*

Just an ordinary priest. The streets of Jerusalem were full of them. Depending on the translation, his name is spelled "Zacharias," "Zachariah," even "Zachary." Same guy. Zechariah was not only a good man; he was also God's man, descended from a long line of holy servants.

> …who belonged to the priestly division of Abijah;…
> *Luke 1:5*

Abijah was just one of twenty-four divisions,[1] so there were *lots* of priests. Since the time of Aaron, their duties included handling various offerings, giving thanks, and singing praises at the gates of God's dwelling place.[2] A worthy calling, though with so many priests, few were singled out for ministry within the temple's Holy Place.

Now that we have Zechariah sorted out, here's the woman we've been eager to meet.

> …his wife Elizabeth was also a descendant of Aaron.
> *Luke 1:5*

A popular name, much loved through the centuries. My mother was an Elizabeth, I'm one too, and so is my daughter-in-law, though each generation picked a different nickname: Betty, Liz, and Beth. The meaning remains the same: "God's promise" or "oath of God."

Like her husband, Elizabeth was in Aaron's lineage, which made her a fine catch since marrying a woman of priestly ancestry was a special blessing.[3] Among her many tasks Elizabeth kept her husband's priestly garments in good repair and welcomed visitors into their home to discuss temple matters.[4]

We know this couple. We've seen them at church, exchanged smiles in the parking lot. Happily married people, busily serving the Lord, always doing good.

> Both of them were righteous in the sight of God, observing all the Lord's commands and decrees blamelessly. *Luke 1:6*

They lived "honorably before God" (MSG) and humbly as well, knowing the Lord alone was their source of righteousness. It may sound as if Elizabeth and her husband were obedient and so earned God's approval, but, in truth, it was the other way around. God's power and strength at work in their lives made it possible for them to do the right thing in the first place.

The same is true for us, of course. Though it's tempting to praise people for their goodness, it's better to praise the One who made them. "For we are God's handiwork, created in Christ Jesus to do good works, which God prepared in advance for us to do."[5]

After such cheery news about Elizabeth and her hubby in the opening verses, it's time for the other shoe to drop. When God's blessings are piled on our heads, it's easy to be faithful.

The real test comes when disappointment calls and sorrow pulls up a chair.

> But they were childless… *Luke 1:7*

Oh no. Not these two godly souls?

Afraid so. Even with all their goodness and righteousness, sadness had crept into their home. In their world children were seen as God's reward for faithful service.[6] We can guess the desperate questions that threaded through their minds as each year went by without a child in their arms. *Are we not faithful enough, Lord? Have we dishonored you in some way?*

Whenever they heard the psalmist's words "the fruit of the womb is a divine reward,"[7] Zechariah and Elizabeth must have steeled themselves, hiding their pain, even as they avoided sidelong glances from their neighbors.

> …because Elizabeth was not able to conceive,…
> *Luke 1:7*

In days of old the woman bore full responsibility. "Elisabeth's infertility" (PHILLIPS) was the problem. She was the one marked as "barren" (ASV). How often had Elizabeth heard that stark word whispered as she passed by? Some women surely had pity in their eyes, others a certain disdain, wondering what

Elizabeth had done to displease God. Whenever she joined them at the well early in the evening, the women's lively chatter about sons and grandsons must have faded into an awkward silence.

In the eyes of her neighbors, Elizabeth "had failed at the most basic level."[8] A wife was expected to give her husband sons and so maintain the honor of his name.[9] The consequences for not doing so could be grave: disfavor, humiliation, divorce.[10]

My heart goes out to Elizabeth, just as I ache for every couple who has longed for children only to have their hopes dashed.

"Though disappointed and quietly suffering, Elizabeth held on to God's promises and clung to the fact that she was God's daughter, all the while waiting, praying, and listening."

—SHERRY

A woman in her early thirties confessed to me, "Apparently my husband and I cannot have children." Since they have yet to conceive, she fears it might never happen—a logical assumption based on solid evidence. Still, that word *apparently* is very telling. Faith is believing what isn't seen, what isn't apparent. This wise young woman is quietly leaving a door open for a miracle.

Elizabeth needed a miracle too. She was not only barren; she was also past her prime, and so was her man.

> …and they were both very old. *Luke 1:7*

We don't know their ages, whether forty or sixty or eighty. We know only that Elizabeth and Zechariah were "well stricken in years" (ASV). More to the point, they were "too old to have children" (GOD'S WORD), just like the patriarch Abraham, and his wife, Sarah. We know how *that* story ended: with a baby in ninety-year-old Sarah's arms!

The stage was set for God to intervene and make the impossible possible. I get chills even thinking about it, don't you? Christmas is all about miracles. The first one is ready to unfold.

> Once when Zechariah's division was on duty and he was serving as priest before God,… *Luke 1:8*

Since priests didn't have a retirement age,[11] Zechariah was still performing his priestly duties when an unexpected blessing came his way.

> …he was chosen by lot, according to the custom of the priesthood,… *Luke 1:9*

This business of casting lots—rather like throwing dice—doesn't sound very spiritual, but that's how priests determined God's will. Regardless of the method, Sovereign God selected Zechariah for this assignment.

> …to go into the temple of the Lord and burn incense.
> *Luke 1:9*

Because there were so many priests to choose from, this would have been the high point of Zechariah's ministry, literally a once-in-a-lifetime opportunity to offer sweet incense at the altar. According to the Law of Moses, a priest "must burn fragrant incense on the altar every morning when he tends the lamps. He must burn incense again when he lights the lamps at twilight so incense will burn regularly before the LORD for the generations to come."[12]

> And when the time for the burning of incense came,
> all the assembled worshipers were praying outside.
> *Luke 1:10*

So how many were present "at the hour of the perfume" (YLT)? We're told a "whole multitude" (ESV) gathered to pray, though not everyone in Jerusalem came. Just "pious Jews who loved to be near the temple when sacrifices were offered."[13]

Elizabeth was surely among them, stationed with the others in the Court of Women, all "silently lifting up their hearts to God in prayer."[14] It was quiet enough in the open courtyard to hear the tinkling of the bells around the hem of the high priest's sky-blue robe as he and several other priests led Zechariah into the Holy Place to burn the sacred incense.

Her husband's big moment had finally come. How proud Elizabeth must have been! She'd not given Zechariah a son, but she'd provided constant support during their many years together. You can be sure Elizabeth did her part that day in the Court of Women, perhaps whispering the words of David: "May my prayer be set before you like incense."[15]

"Elizabeth didn't take matters into her own hands.
She trusted her future to God's capable hands."

—MARBARA

Another elderly woman, far older than Elizabeth, was no doubt present since "she never left the temple."[16] We've not met Anna yet, but we will in a later chapter. For now we can picture her among these devout women, worshiping God.

Meanwhile, the other priests withdrew from the Holy Place, leaving Zechariah alone to perform the offering.[17] Since he had never done this task before, if he was nervous, even a little jumpy, no one would have blamed him. He was expected to burn incense each morning and evening for a full week[18] in the very presence of the Lord Almighty.

Before him stood the altar, made of wood and covered with pure gold. Twice as tall as it was wide, the waist-high altar had a golden horn on each corner. On one side stood the golden table with the bread of the Presence.[19] And on the other, the golden lampstand.

Everything was in place. All was in readiness.

But Zechariah was not alone.

> Then an angel of the Lord appeared to him,
> standing at the right side of the altar of incense.
> *Luke 1:11*

Oh my. Even serving God in his holy temple, Zechariah was unprepared for something holy to happen. Yet it did. God swept away the cloud of incense and made his presence known by way of an angel.

> When Zechariah saw him, he was startled...
> *Luke 1:12*

Who wouldn't be? His response is captured in "a word of deep emotion,"[20] meant to convey everything he was thinking and feeling: "amazed" (NIrV), "bewildered" (KNOX), "alarmed"

(GNT), and "shaken" (NLT). We're right there with him, imagining this heavenly creature close enough to touch.

Zechariah knew about God's messengers, but he'd never encountered one before, nor had any priest of his acquaintance. For more than four hundred years, God had not spoken a fresh word to his people, Malachi having been the last prophet, about 435 BC.[21]

Now an angel stood beside the altar of incense. *An angel.* "The thin veil between the seen and the unseen had been rent for an instant."[22] No wonder Zechariah was "paralyzed" (MSG).

> …and was gripped with fear. *Luke 1:12*

We know from descriptions found elsewhere in the Bible that angels are bigger than life, whiter than snow, and scarier than all get-out. Maybe that's why Elizabeth's husband was "terrified at the sight" (CJB).

> But the angel said to him: "Do not be afraid, Zechariah;…" *Luke 1:13*

The angel wasn't scolding Zechariah; he was comforting him. "Fear not" (KJV), he said. "Calm down!" (VOICE). I need these words embroidered on a pillow, framed on my wall, scribbled across my mouse pad—anywhere I might see them—to remind me that God is in charge, God can be trusted, and God does everything out of love. *Fear not. Calm down.* Why do we fear the worst from God, when he loves us completely and always gives us what is best?

"Even the things we don't understand are a display of the goodness of God."

—STEPH

"…your prayer has been heard." *Luke 1:13*

Good news indeed. But *which* prayer of Zechariah's? The one about Elizabeth? about her infertility? If so, his next question might have been "What took you so long?" Surely this righteous couple had prayed for the gift of children for decades. Why the delay?

According to God's magnificent plan, the perfect time had only now arrived. And if Zechariah's prayer went beyond the personal—if it was for the redemption of Israel, a fitting petition for a devout priest—God had heard that request as well and was ready with an answer.

The angel's next words must have shaken Zechariah to the core.

"Your wife Elizabeth will bear you a son, and you are
to call him John." *Luke 1:13*

A son? A son! Zechariah had waited the whole of his life
to hear those words. And this holy messenger really cut to the
chase. So much information packed into one brief sentence.

"Your wife Elizabeth" made it clear that Zechariah was not
to seek out some younger, more fertile woman (shades of Abram
and Hagar in Genesis 16). Elizabeth was the one chosen by
God. "Will bear you" was a promise that left no room for
doubt. Not it *might* happen; it *will* happen. Every conception
has a touch of the miraculous—this one far more than most.
Elizabeth barren? Not anymore.

"A baby boy" (ERV) was always welcome in ancient Israel,
where sons were "like arrows in the hand of a warrior."[23] "You
must call his name John" (AMP) assured this frightened father-
to-be that he would have the honor of conferring upon his son
the name John, meaning "the Lord is gracious."[24]

While Zechariah was still reeling from the thought of having an heir, the angel told him more about this extraordinary
child to come. It was an impressive list, a veritable top ten,
spelled out in Luke 1:14–17:

He will be a joy and delight to you.
He will cause many to rejoice because of his birth.

He will be great in the sight of the Lord.

He will never touch wine or strong drink.

He will be filled with the Holy Spirit even before he is born.

He will bring back many people of Israel to the Lord their
    God.

He will go before the Lord in the spirit and power of
    Elijah.

He will turn the hearts of parents to their children.

He will turn the hearts of the disobedient to the wisdom
    of the righteous.

He will make ready a people prepared for the Lord.

The last one is how we best know John, who would one day
be known as John the Baptist: "A voice of one calling in the
wilderness, 'Prepare the way for the Lord, make straight paths
for him.' "[25] Imagine hearing all those accolades about your son
even before he was conceived! Everything a godly parent could
hope for.

Our father-to-be should have been joyful and grateful. Instead he was doubtful. Zechariah believed in God, but he wasn't
certain the Lord could overcome an obstacle like Elizabeth's
infertility. No, the man wanted proof.

> Zechariah asked the angel, "How can I be sure of
> this?" *Luke 1:18*

Really? Wasn't the appearance of an angel enough? This elderly priest should have known God was trustworthy. Instead, he asked, "By what sign am I to be assured of this?" (KNOX).

It's easy for me to find fault with this man—and hard to admit how many times I've done the same thing. *Show me, Lord. Convince me.* Beneath my bravado hides a frightened child. *Do you really mean it, Father? Do you love me that much?*

"I understand Zechariah's uncertainty. I fear I may be keeping God from working with my own doubts and fears."

— STACY

Like Zechariah, we sometimes forget whom we're talking to. The promises of God seem "too good to be true—too hard to believe!"[26] Yet *believing* is what Christmas is all about. Believing Jesus is the Son of God. Believing he was born of a virgin. Believing he came to earth to rescue us from our doubts and save us from our sins.

Zechariah, however, was a practical fellow. After asking the angel, "Do you expect me to believe this?" (MSG), he justified his lackluster faith with facts.

"I am an old man..." *Luke 1:18*

From Zechariah's viewpoint, fathering a child at his age would be impossible. He was also worried about his "old woman" (MSG).

"…and my wife is well along in years." *Luke 1:18*

Scholars believe Elizabeth was menopausal, perhaps forty.[27] Whatever her age, in her husband's opinion she was "beyond her childbearing years" (GOD'S WORD). But she wasn't beyond the touch of God, the Creator of all things, the Author of life. His own Son would later say, "With God all things are possible."[28] Why would a person's age matter to our eternal God?

The Lord hadn't forgotten Elizabeth, nor had he tarried in answering her prayer without a good purpose. He chose her—an older woman with an unproven womb—in order to display his power, his might, his authority. And he blessed her to honor her faithfulness.

The truth is, God's strength is fully revealed when our strength is fully depleted. His power is made perfect in our weakness.[29] He's a refuge for the oppressed; he's a stronghold in times of trouble.[30] He is God, and believe me, he's got this!

An old man filled with doubt and fear was about to find

out just how powerful a God he served. And his wife, Elizabeth, praying with her sisters of the faith, would soon discover that, whatever her age, she was still precious in God's sight.

As are you, beloved. Absolutely.

Two

Let all mortal flesh keep silence,
And with fear and trembling stand;
Ponder nothing earthly minded,
For with blessing in his hand,
Christ our God to earth descendeth
Our full homage to demand.

—Translated by Gerard Moultrie,
"Let All Mortal Flesh Keep Silence," 1864

Let All Mortal Flesh
Keep Silence

Shh. I heard that sound all through my childhood and for good reason. I was either talking too loudly or talking too much. However gentle the correction, I chafed at having to be quiet. Only as I matured did I finally learn the value of silence.

Sometimes our speechlessness is born of reverence. Sometimes, of fear. For Zechariah, silence would soon become a holy necessity. While Elizabeth waited and prayed in the Court of Women, her husband experienced the Lord's mighty power in an up-close and personal way as he stood before the altar of incense.

The angel said to him, "I am Gabriel." *Luke 1:19*

Why save his name until this moment? Because Gabriel means "Strength of God."[1] It was time for Zechariah to stop thinking in human terms and get the big picture.

"I stand in the presence of God,..." *Luke 1:19*

Zechariah had to be trembling in his sandals. Gabriel is "the sentinel of God" (MSG), "the messenger who inhabits God's presence" (VOICE). He is with God. *With God.* In that Holy Place. *With Zechariah.*

Suddenly I have the urge to slip off my shoes, bow my head, fall to my knees. *Holy, holy, holy.*

> "...and I have been sent to speak to you and to tell you this good news." *Luke 1:19*

The angel came to "evangelize" (WYC) Zechariah, the usual term for "preaching the gospel."[2] We have no record of Gabriel speaking to others during this visitation. Only Zechariah, whose name means "God remembers." The Almighty's presence was proof of that remembrance. Alas, Zechariah had already voiced his doubts. It seems Gabriel had heard enough from this priest.

> "And now you will be silent and not able to speak..." *Luke 1:20*

Strong words, strongly spoken. "Now listen!" (HCSB). How could poor Zechariah do otherwise? When he opened his mouth, no sound came out. Just as Gabriel promised, Zechariah had "no power of speech" (KNOX).

Many scholars believe he also lost the ability to hear,[3] in part because the Greek word *kophos* can also mean "deaf."[4] And later his neighbors "made signs"[5] to Zechariah, suggesting he couldn't hear their voices. When Gabriel told him, "You shall live in silence" (PHILLIPS), he meant it.

"…until the day this happens,…" *Luke 1:20*

Uh-oh. Until the day *what* happens? What "shall come to pass" (ASV)? However righteous Zechariah was, he had doubted this holy messenger and trusted his own opinion. *I am old. My wife is old. A child is not possible.* Would God still honor his promise, still give Zechariah a son?

"…because you did not believe my words,…" *Luke 1:20*

When Gabriel pointed out Zechariah's sin, the old priest surely feared all was lost. Yet in the same breath, the angel announced the best news Zechariah could hope for. Those words, those heavenly promises about his son, would still be fulfilled.

"…which will come true at their appointed time."
Luke 1:20

God be praised! Despite Zechariah's doubts, fears, and disbelief, he would hold a son in his arms. Gabriel didn't tell him when this would occur, but he didn't need to. Zechariah's faith had been fully restored. He knew it would happen "on time—*God's* time" (MSG).

The loss of speech wasn't punishment; it was the proof Zechariah had asked for, the assurance of God's power. *If I can take away your voice, can I not also give you a son?*

> *"Many times I've looked at a bad circumstance as God's punishment. Maybe it was just God reminding me that he is with me and he's working out his master plan for my life!"*
> —TINA

Zechariah's silence may have served another purpose. Perhaps the world was not ready to learn about his son yet. And Elizabeth, more than anyone else, deserved to hear the good news first.

With his angelic mission accomplished, Gabriel disappeared as quickly as he'd arrived, leaving Zechariah in a quandary. He *had* to speak. Wasn't the crowd expecting him to pronounce a blessing over them?[6]

> Meanwhile, the people were waiting for Zechariah
> and wondering why he stayed so long in the temple.
> *Luke 1:21*

The incense offering was a brief ceremony, so naturally they were "bewildered at his delay" (ojb). Had the crowd stopped praying and started murmuring? We can be sure Elizabeth's eyes were turned toward the entrance to the Holy Place, watching for her husband to emerge and proclaim the blessing of Aaron: "The LORD bless you and keep you; the LORD make his face shine on you and be gracious to you; the LORD turn his face toward you and give you peace."[7] But Zechariah didn't give the assembly a blessing. He gave them silence.

> When he came out, he could not speak to them.
> *Luke 1:22*

We know why. He was *illem,* the Hebrew word for "mute." Out of habit his lips might have been moving, but nothing came out. Instead he gestured wildly, trying to explain himself.

> They realized he had seen a vision in the temple, for
> he kept making signs to them but remained unable to
> speak. *Luke 1:22*

What precisely had happened to Zechariah in the Holy Place was unclear to them, but the people knew he'd seen "something special from God" (NLV) as he "made signs to them with his hands" (GNT). Nothing formal, not true sign language. I suspect it was closer to the exaggerated gestures we use when we play charades or our bumbling efforts when visiting a foreign country.

During one family vacation we pulled into a small post office outside Toulouse. Not knowing the French word for *postage stamp,* I formed a square with my fingers, then pretended to press imaginary stamps onto the corners of my postcards, before joining my hands like wings and flapping them toward the door. Airmail, right?

My family couldn't stop laughing. The postal workers are *still* laughing.

That brings us to Zechariah. What did he shape with his hands? An angelic being? A babe in his arms? His future son's top ten list of attributes? Whatever Zechariah demonstrated to the crowd, they were convinced he'd seen a vision and been struck speechless. No calling in sick for Zechariah, though. He still had his religious duties to fulfill even though he had no voice and was deaf.[8]

All that week Zechariah likely remained at the temple in a special apartment provided for the priests. Elizabeth might have returned each morning and evening to pray, then lodged with close friends or family members in Jerusalem. Did she and her husband ever have a moment alone? Zechariah must have been eager to convey the angel's pronouncement, whether that meant spelling out words in the sand or scratching the news onto a wax tablet. And Elizabeth must have been dying to know more about what had happened in the temple.

An *angel*? A *baby*? How was it possible?

Hard to guess who was more frustrated, husband or wife, as they tried to communicate without speaking or hearing. We can see Elizabeth gesturing right along with Zechariah, alternately smiling and frowning as she grasped some nugget of information, only to be stymied by another. This much would have been easily imparted: *You are going to have a child, Elizabeth. You are going to have our son!*

> When his time of service was completed, he returned home. *Luke 1:23*

At last they were alone and beneath their own roof. Elizabeth could perform her wifely duties, praying a child might be conceived just as the angel had foretold.

"I sometimes forget what a significant part Elizabeth plays in the Christmas story. She reminds us that God's timing is always best."

—KIRRA

We have no record of her doubting, though a few practicalities did need to be addressed. Had her flow ceased some time earlier? Or did Elizabeth still follow her monthly calendar with care, not wanting to miss what the local midwives insisted was the most opportune time?

She had never been fertile before. Was she now?

In the days and weeks that followed, Elizabeth probably walked from one corner of their home to the other, praying aloud, begging God to bless her womb. She would have avoided green vegetables, salt, and fats since first-century women knew how troublesome those foods could be to an unborn child.[9]

Dared she dream of a tiny hand latching on to her forefinger? A toothless smile in a cherub's round face? A plaintive cry in the night, music to her ears alone?

If Zechariah was right. *If* God was merciful.

> After this his wife Elizabeth became pregnant…
> *Luke 1:24*

I love how the Bible presents miracles in such a matter-of-fact way. *Then this happened. Just as God had said it would.* What we call miraculous, God calls business as usual. "It wasn't long" (MSG) before "Elizabeth conceived" (ESV) and was "expecting a baby" (CEV).

Thanks be to God!

Had I been Elizabeth, I would have run from one friend's house to the next, spreading the good news. But she did just the opposite. Elizabeth stayed out of view, and "the miracle remained a secret."[10]

> ...and for five months remained in seclusion.
> *Luke 1:24*

That's right. For the first twenty-two weeks of her pregnancy, Elizabeth didn't "leave the house" (CEV) or "go out in public" (GOD'S WORD). Was it fear that kept her under wraps? Was she waiting for further proof? Women who desperately want to be pregnant can convince themselves they feel queasy in the morning or their breasts are more sensitive or their energy is depleted.

No scholar or teacher can be certain why Elizabeth "hid herself" (DRA), but many have ventured a guess. Perhaps she wanted to "avoid gawking neighbors."[11] My mother was pregnant with me at age forty-three, which was highly unusual back in the day. She confessed to me that she was embarrassed throughout her pregnancy and avoided going anywhere. Except bridge club, of course.

Maybe Elizabeth wanted to wait "until she was so obviously pregnant that no-one could accuse her of lying."[12] Could be she cherished the time alone with God or wanted to care for her deaf and mute husband. However temporary his condition, Zechariah must have struggled with his new limitations.

On the positive side, with Elizabeth sequestered in their house, "no-one could accuse her of sexual misdemeanor."[13] The child would assuredly belong to Zechariah the priest. Perhaps Elizabeth wanted to treasure the good news until she was ready for the big reveal. "Better to savor in private her precious secret rather than to attempt explanations that no one would accept."[14]

> *"Despite the doubts she must have faced through the years, Elizabeth gave her all, and the Lord gave her a blessing beyond belief."*
>
> —LIZ

Maybe she was simply avoiding all the unwanted advice that relatives and friends love to dish out. Theories abound, but only Elizabeth herself could tell us the truth. Exiled by choice with a husband who could neither speak nor hear, she turned to the One who gladly listened to her as she poured out her hopes and fears, her joys and concerns. "Years of suffering had brought her very near to the heart of God."[15]

Why that specific length of time, though? Not two full trimesters. Five months.

Here's my take.

First-time mothers usually sense the quickening—the first movement of the child, the certainty of life—between the eighteenth and twentieth week of pregnancy.[16] In this context the word *quick* doesn't mean "swift"; it means "alive." I remember exactly where I was and what I was doing when I felt that first tiny shift. Even with all the other symptoms, the quickening makes everything *real*.

Elizabeth might have been waiting for that absolute assurance.

The second clue for mothers-to-be is an expanding waistline. Every woman's body is different, but by the end of the fifth month, Elizabeth's baby bump was bound to show. Did they have maternity fashions two thousand years ago? Maybe women simply belted their tunics higher.

This we know: when the time came for Elizabeth's self-imposed silence to end, she spoke with boldness and gratitude.

"The Lord has done this for me," she said. *Luke 1:25*

We can see her stepping across the threshold into the bright light of day, hiding nothing. "This is the Lord's doing" (CEB), she told her neighbors. Zechariah had also done his loving duty by her, just as he had throughout their marriage. But Elizabeth knew the real source of the babe inside her: "Children are a gift from the LORD."[17]

"It seems as if all of my friends and family members are mothers. I am struggling with continuing to find hope in God alone. Elizabeth's story is so encouraging."
—NICOLE

Elizabeth couldn't take credit for being fertile any more than Zechariah could take a bow for being virile. As in all things, God alone deserves the glory. We can hear the exaltation in Elizabeth's voice. She was barren no more. Though her husband was silent, God had spoken.

"In these days..." *Luke 1:25*

More like months, but we know what she meant: "Since you last saw me..." "While I've been away from you..." Elizabeth described this season when the Lord was "visiting me at his own time" (KNOX) in a very personal way. Only a woman with a deep and abiding relationship with God could make such a claim: *I have been with God these many months. And he has been with me.*

"...he has shown his favor..." *Luke 1:25*

When we first met Elizabeth, we learned she was "righteous,"[18] meaning God's favor was already upon her. But now his favor was showing. It was visible. Undeniable. "He decided to help me" (ERV), Elizabeth explained. "How kind the Lord is!" (NLT). So kind that he changed everything: her body, her calling, her future, and her reputation.

> "…and taken away my disgrace among the people."
> *Luke 1:25*

"I have suffered" (PHILLIPS), she admitted, but her "public disgrace" (CJB) was finally over. "Now people will stop thinking there is something wrong with me" (ERV). We know there was never anything wrong with Elizabeth. She'd made room in her heart, body, and soul for a miracle. And God had the situation well in hand.

> *"In my own heart, do I always make room for him? Do I push aside my busyness, my fears, my worries, my wants to make room for him here? with me? in me?"*
> —SUSAN

Through all her years of feeling less-than, Elizabeth had worshiped a more-than God. Now she intended to give him the glory for it.

What's the opposite of disgrace? Ah. Grace. God filled her with his favor, his mercy, his loving-kindness. Then he filled her with a son from the seed of Zechariah. And he didn't quit there. When we meet Elizabeth again, she will be filled with joy, with praise, and with a gift that could only come from God, "who is able to do immeasurably more than all we ask or imagine, according to his power that is at work within us."[19]

His power in us. Breathtaking, isn't it?

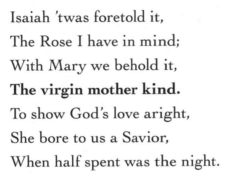

Three

Isaiah 'twas foretold it,
The Rose I have in mind;
With Mary we behold it,
The virgin mother kind.
To show God's love aright,
She bore to us a Savior,
When half spent was the night.

—Translated by Theodore Baker,
"Lo, How a Rose E'er Blooming," 1894

The Virgin
Mother Kind

*H*er name is synonymous with innocence, purity, devotion. And her calling was like no other woman's before or since: she gave birth to the Savior of the world.

Already I'm stepping back, putting some distance between myself and this Wonder Girl. Young. Chaste. Submissive. I am none of those things.

You were once, the Lord gently reminds me. *When you were twelve and sang "Morning Star" from the choir loft at Christmastime. Do you remember that sweet child? Because I do.*

I quickly close my eyes, feeling the sting of tears. It was a very long time ago. But, yes, I remember those innocent days. Perhaps you do too. Our hearts were untried, and our bodies were untouched. We stood on tiptoe, gazing at the future, wondering what it might be like to fall in love, to marry, to surrender to a husband's embrace.

That's where we find Mary.

In the sixth month of Elizabeth's pregnancy,...
Luke 1:26

This wasn't the sixth month of the year; it was "six months after Elizabeth knew she was to become a mother" (NLV). Imagine the Lord using an expectant mother's growing waistline to measure time! Never doubt for a moment that women matter to the Almighty.

Elizabeth only recently had come out of hiding. "One month later" (CEV) her young kinswoman Mary was about to have her own angelic encounter.

...God sent the angel Gabriel to Nazareth, a town in Galilee,... *Luke 1:26*

We last met Gabriel when he appeared to Elizabeth's husband, Zechariah. Now God's messenger was headed to Nazareth, a small village in a narrow, secluded valley away from the main trade routes.[1]

In Mary's time barely one hundred people called Nazareth home. They were hardworking folk. Laborers, shepherds, tradesmen, farmers.[2] Some lived in limestone and clay-walled homes[3] with flat rooftops, inner courtyards, and small, square windows high above the dusty street. The poorest families dwelled in caves.

Little wonder that when he first met Jesus, Nathanael

scoffed, "Nazareth! Can anything good come from there?"[4] Yet God considered this insignificant village worthy of his attention. He sent Gabriel there, bearing good news for a girl who stood on the cusp of womanhood.

> ...to a virgin... *Luke 1:27*

She was "a maiden" (WYC), that is to say, "a woman who had never had a man" (NLV). Even so, a future husband waited in the wings for Mary.

> ...pledged to be married to a man named Joseph,...
> *Luke 1:27*

Don't let words such as "engaged" (CEV), "betrothed" (ASV), and "promised" (GNT) throw you. Mary and Joseph were as good as wed. Theirs was a written and legally binding oath, witnessed by their neighbors at a formal ceremony in the village square.[5] According to tradition, Joseph would have presented a gift to Mary and said, "By this, thou art set apart for me according to the laws of Moses and of Israel."[6]

The only way to break such a vow was through a formal divorce, and those were uncommon. However, if one of the betrothed proved unfaithful...well, suppose we circle back to that later in our story.

> *"How amazing to find stories in the Bible of others going through problems like ours, and how wonderful to see God meet them in the midst of their distressing circumstances."*
>
> —ELIZABETH

Mary was very young—twelve to twelve and a half, perhaps even younger.[7] Girls were betrothed as soon as they could bear children, both to protect their innocence and to allow for many healthy years of childbearing. Babies having babies, we'd say today. But two thousand years ago that was how things were done.

Young men waited to marry until they were capable of supporting a wife and so were usually several years older and established in a trade.[8] A carpenter like Joseph would have spent his days making doors and shutters, cartwheels and plows for his neighbors[9] while preparing a home for Mary as she readied her wedding clothes.[10]

They were not yet living under the same roof—a full year often stretched between engagement and marriage.[11] To protect her reputation and Joseph's, Mary had to steer clear of any social gatherings and behave as a chaste and proper bride-to-be.[12]

So why didn't the Lord select a young woman who wasn't betrothed and spare Mary and Joseph all the angst that surely followed when she became pregnant? Because God's Son would need an earthly father. And Joseph was the man for the job, thanks to his loyal heart and his royal roots.

…a descendant of David. *Luke 1:27*

The gospel of Matthew lays it out for us: "This is the genealogy of Jesus the Messiah the son of David, the son of Abraham."[13] A master gardener, God had pruned and watered his Son's family tree from before the beginning of time, numbering the days, weeks, months, years, centuries, and millenniums, until the moment came to send Gabriel on a mission.

The virgin's name was Mary. *Luke 1:27*

A second reminder of her innocence. One meaning of her name is "bitter," perhaps a hint of her sorrow to come. Being loved by God would not spare her the heartaches and tragedies of life. Yet in the Bible we never see any bitterness in her words or actions. Impressive, no?

She was "likely uneducated and probably came from a poor family."[14] Like the child she bore, who "had no beauty or majesty to attract us to him, nothing in his appearance that we should desire him,"[15] Mary, I suspect, was rather plain in appearance. Certainly in her dress and speech, perhaps also in her face and figure, she was unremarkable.

God didn't choose Mary because she was unique. Mary was unique because God chose her. He knew her tender heart, her trusting nature, her abiding faith, her humble spirit. He who formed Mary in her mother's womb would soon form his Son in Mary's womb.

Once again the Lord pulled back the invisible curtain between heaven and earth and ushered in Gabriel to deliver the happy news.

The angel went to her... *Luke 1:28*

We're not told what Mary was doing at the time, but I'm fairly certain she wasn't staring up at the skies over Nazareth, watching for a heavenly visitor. Gabriel simply "appeared to her" (NLT)—unheralded and unexpected, from her viewpoint—while she was pressing olives, baking bread, or trimming her lamp.

In the same way, while we go about our daily tasks, God's divine plan is unfolding. At any given moment our lives could change dramatically. No surprise to God, yet a big surprise to us. That's what we find happening here.

And consider this: the angel appeared to Mary first, not to her husband-to-be, Joseph. "She had no status or honor apart from him,"[16] yet Gabriel came to Mary—further proof of how much God values women.

...and said, "Greetings,..." *Luke 1:28*

We smile, imagining Gabriel saying, "Greetings, earthling!" Though perhaps "Rejoice" (CEB), a common salutation of the day, or "Hail" (ASV) was better suited to a heavenly messenger. From the start it was clear that Gabriel came bearing good news: "Peace be with you!" (GNT).

Although you may be picturing a huge, winged creature, Gabriel probably looked like an ordinary man.[17] He isn't described as big, bright, or shining. And Mary wasn't noticeably frightened by his appearance. Gabriel's words, however, gave her pause.

"...you who are highly favored!" *Luke 1:28*

"*Shalom,* favored lady!" (CJB). That statement would get a girl's attention, all right. In Latin the beautiful phrase reads *gratia plena,* meaning "one who has been filled with grace."[18] An exclamation point doesn't appear in the original Greek, but it definitely captures the energy and excitement of the moment. "You are truly blessed!" (CEV).

"God has a plan for me and for you, just as he did for Mary. In some way we are all highly favored."
—CATHY

Mary was full of God's grace simply because God chose to bless her. We have no description of her being holy or pious or deserving. She was a virgin, yes, but not perfect, not without sin. For Jesus to be fully the Son of Man, his mother had to be fully human.

What made Mary worthy of her calling was not *her* virtue; it was God's virtue. That's why her story gives every woman a generous measure of hope. God takes us as we are and uses us as he will, for our good and for his glory. Talk about being "endued with grace!" (AMP).

Now get ready for this one.

> "The Lord is with you." *Luke 1:28*

This wasn't a blessing, like the ones we often find in Scripture: "May the LORD show you kindness,"[19] and "May the LORD your God be with you."[20] This was a statement of fact. Not God will be or may be or could be with her. Gabriel said, "*ADONAI* is with you!" (CJB).

Did Mary have any sense of this? A shimmer of light, a tremor in the air, the weight of his glory resting on her shoulders? Remember, if Gabriel stood in the presence of God,[21] so did she.

> Mary was greatly troubled at his words and wondered what kind of greeting this might be. *Luke 1:29*

She was "thoroughly shaken" (MSG) and "very perplexed" (NASB), which in the Lizzie Revised Version means she was "totally flipped out." Who could fault her? A heavenly being had just showed up and announced, "The Lord is with you!" (CEB).

On the heels of this astounding news, Gabriel offered a word of comfort.

> But the angel said to her, "Do not be afraid, Mary;…"
> *Luke 1:30*

How like the Lord to identify our fears and hasten to ease them. Notice that Gabriel called her by name: "Mary, you have nothing to fear" (MSG). God knew her name just as he knows ours. A pastor of a large church may not know the name of every person sitting in the pews. But God does. Every one.

> "…you have found favor with God." *Luke 1:30*

A moment earlier the angel told Mary she was "highly favored." Why remind her that God had showered her with his "free, spontaneous, absolute favor and loving-kindness" (AMP)? Maybe she missed it the first time. Like when my doctor gives me oral instructions, then provides written ones too. Otherwise, if I'm worried or nervous, I may miss something important.

Gabriel's words make this blessing sound like a guarantee.

Not God will extend his grace to you someday if you're good, if you're worthy. Grace was already happening. "God is honoring you" (CEB). "God loves you dearly" (PHILLIPS). His mighty power was at work, preparing her body, soothing her soul.

Then came the news that changed the world—hers first of all. As Eugene Peterson phrased it, "God has a surprise for you" (MSG).

"You will conceive…" *Luke 1:31*

Her heart must have skipped a beat. Mary was still getting used to the idea of becoming a wife. Now it seemed mother-hood was a certainty: "You will become pregnant" (CJB). But when? She'd not spent time alone with Joseph and wouldn't do so until they were truly wed.

You will conceive. Would it be next year, then? Sooner?

"…and give birth to a son,…" *Luke 1:31*

Not just a child, Mary. "You are going to be the mother of a son" (PHILLIPS). For a fleeting moment she might have thought of Joseph and how pleased he would be to have an heir.

"…and you are to call him Jesus." *Luke 1:31*

Jesus. We can almost hear Mary gasp as the meaning of his name began to stir something inside her. "God saves." *Can it be possible?*

"He will be great…" *Luke 1:32*

Every mother believes the son or daughter in her womb will be special. Only one woman in history has heard so exalted a description of her unborn son as the statements that follow. Even more powerful words such as *splendor, majesty, honor,* and *glory* would be used to describe him. In the next breath Mary learned why.

"…and will be called the Son of the Most High."
Luke 1:32

Oh, Mary. *The Most High?* Who else could that be but the Almighty?

"The Lord God will give him the throne of his father David,…" *Luke 1:32*

Did her knees grow weak as the truth sank in? *Lord. God. King.* "For centuries Jewish women had hoped that one of them might become the mother of the Messiah."[22] The fact that Mary was still standing, still breathing, still listening was a tribute to her courage.

> "...and he will reign over Jacob's descendants forever; his kingdom will never end." *Luke 1:33*

Not just king for a decade or two. Forever and ever, amen, just as the psalmist recorded: "I will establish his line forever, his throne as long as the heavens endure."[23]

Mary's response is one of my favorites in Scripture. It's honest and thoughtful and humble. She didn't have a million questions. She just had one.

> "How will this be," Mary asked the angel, "since I am a virgin?" *Luke 1:34*

Not "How will my son be great and the Son of God and king forever?" No, Mary was back at the angel's opening promise: "And in your womb you will conceive" (OJB). It's the third mention of her virginity in this scene, and it came from Mary, the one person who knew the truth on that score. Her question was valid: "How shall this be done?" (DRA).

She wasn't like Zechariah, asking for proof. Mary didn't doubt God could manage this miracle. She just wanted to know *how,* "seeing I know not a man?" (asv). Young as she was, we can imagine her wide-eyed exclamation: "How can this happen? I am not married!" (cev).

> The angel answered,… *Luke 1:35*

Gabriel didn't only proclaim; he also listened and responded. Clearly it's okay—more than okay—to ask God how he will accomplish something. Even if his answer is "Trust me," we can be sure he hears us.

But this answer, I confess, steals my breath.

> …"The Holy Spirit will come on you, and the power
> of the Most High will overshadow you." *Luke 1:35*

Mary was so young, so naive. This description might have terrified her.

Centuries later scholars still aren't certain what it meant for God's power to "hover over" (msg) her "like a shining cloud" (amp). Was it similar to when "the cloud covered the tent of meeting, and the glory of the LORD filled the tabernacle"?[24] Or more like when "darkness was over the surface of the deep, and the Spirit of God was hovering over the waters"?[25]

An aura of mystery surrounds these ancient words. Most translations say only that the Holy Spirit will "come down" (cev) or "come on" (GNT), though this one puts a finer point on things: "The Holy Ghost shall come from above into thee" (WYC).

Well. Okay. We're starting to get the picture, through a glass, darkly. If people tell you they know exactly how Mary received God's Seed, they are filling in the blanks of an enigma too deep for human minds to plumb. What matters is that God was entirely in charge of this process, and his Son would be born because of it.

> "So the holy one to be born will be called the Son of God." *Luke 1:35*

In Mary's time and place, every firstborn male was consecrated to God. This son of hers will *be* God. The Amplified Bible helps us grasp the meaning further: "and so the holy (pure, sinless) Thing (Offspring) which shall be born *of you* will be called the Son of God."

To her credit Mary didn't ask for clarification or press for details. She believed the angel because she believed in the One who had sent him. Nonetheless, Gabriel encouraged her further.

> "Even Elizabeth your relative is going to have a child in her old age, and she who was said to be unable to conceive is in her sixth month." *Luke 1:36*

Elizabeth's conception was remarkable because of her advanced age, but at least her husband was involved in the process! Still, the unexpected news about Mary's kinswoman must have comforted her as she realized that if the miracle of Elizabeth's pregnancy could happen, maybe her own conception wasn't so far-fetched. It also meant Mary would not have to face this nine-month journey alone. She would have a confidante, a listening ear, an experienced woman who could help her.

"First the Lord used Elizabeth, who was 'too old,' then he used Mary, who would be 'too young' by today's standards. At any age we can serve the Lord."

—SHELLY

The angel's next words ring through the ages, having empowered not only Mary but also everyone who has ever read them on a page or heard them spoken.

"For no word from God will ever fail." *Luke 1:37*

There it is: the splendid banner flying over this scene. A truth that answers every doubt, every fear, every question, every concern and is "one of the most reassuring statements in all

Scripture."[26] In each translation the same powerful promise comes through: "Nothing is impossible for God!" (CEV). That's right. "God can do anything!" (NCV).

Sometimes we whisper to ourselves, "No way. That's impossible." For us, perhaps, but not for our heavenly Father. As an angel once said within Sarah's earshot, "Is anything too hard for the LORD?"[27] The obvious answer is *no*.

Then why do we throw up roadblocks when God drives a tank? He can remove any obstacle, overcome any challenge, mow down any opposition. He is the very definition of trustworthy. And he can do anything. *Anything.*

Mary carried Jesus in her body. By the same Holy Spirit, we "carry the risen Lord in our hearts."[28] Nothing is impossible with God residing in us and working through us.

"What might God do in my life if I believed that he really and truly can do the impossible?"

—ELISABETH

The angel had spoken. Now it was Mary's turn. Would she take that leap of faith? For her sake, for our sake?

"I am the Lord's servant," Mary answered.
Luke 1:38

Bless you, Mary. Her first response was to humble herself. Mary knew her place, but even more she knew God's place: all-powerful, all-seeing, all-knowing, and all-loving.

Because of who he is, Mary was able to offer herself to him as a "bondslave" (NASB), a "handmaid" (KJV), "a female slave whose will was not her own."[29] Eugene Peterson puts Mary's vow in terms we can run with: "Yes, I see it all now: I'm the Lord's maid, ready to serve" (MSG).

Think of this young maiden "consciously and willingly joining with the purpose of God to bring salvation to the world."[30] Only God could have provided the faith necessary to take such a huge leap. And leap she did.

"May your word to me be fulfilled." *Luke 1:38*

Young as she was, her words might have sounded more like "Let this thing you have said happen to me!" (ERV). Mary was not only willing; she was clearly eager. *Yes, yes, yes.*

Then the angel left her. *Luke 1:38*

He waited until she was ready. He waited until she was at peace. "Mary was left alone to ponder and to pray, to thrill with inexpressible joy, and to praise with deep humility."[31]

> "The plans I envisioned for my life have not come to fruition, and I have no idea what lies ahead for me. Mary's story gives me hope that God is the God of the impossible. That—zap!—things can change for me too."
>
> —ANN

As a devout young woman, she surely knew the prophecy of Isaiah: "Therefore the Lord himself will give you a sign: The virgin will conceive and give birth to a son, and will call him Immanuel."[32] Did she begin to tremble all over, realizing Isaiah was talking about *her*? A poor girl in a forgotten village? *Immanuel. God with us. God with me!*

One woman in my online Bible study raised the question "What if Mary had said no?" That's why the Lord chose Mary. He knew she would say yes. God did not have Plan A, Plan B, Plan C. Mary was The Plan.

With Gabriel no longer there to comfort and assure her, Mary must have been overwhelmed with the secret she carried inside her heart. How would she explain what she'd heard and seen to her friends, to her parents? No one in Nazareth had ever encountered an angel. How would she make them understand? What if they didn't believe her?

When we meet Mary again, she will be on the move and pregnant. Did the Holy Spirit hover over her the instant she said yes? Or did that sacred moment fall between this scene and the next, shrouded in darkness?

This we know: the miracle was accomplished, and the child was growing, all because an ordinary woman clasped hands with an extraordinary God.

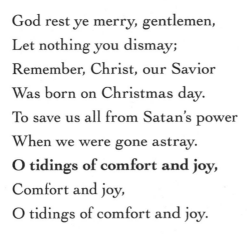

Four

God rest ye merry, gentlemen,
Let nothing you dismay;
Remember, Christ, our Savior
Was born on Christmas day.
To save us all from Satan's power
When we were gone astray.
O tidings of comfort and joy,
Comfort and joy,
O tidings of comfort and joy.

—Traditional English Carol,
"God Rest Ye Merry, Gentlemen," 1760

O Tidings of
Comfort and Joy

When I was pregnant with our firstborn, I carried around a well-marked copy of *What to Expect When You're Expecting,* counting on its practical wisdom to get me through those tumultuous months. With our next child I turned to a close friend who was also expecting her second. We exchanged advice, discussed at length the many joys and discomforts of pregnancy, and cheered each other on as our delivery dates drew near.

If you need encouragement or a listening ear, it's hard to beat a friend who's walking the same path. That brings us to Mary and Elizabeth, who didn't even *expect* to be expecting. It's easy to see why the first person Mary wanted to talk to was her pregnant kinswoman, who shared Mary's faith in a wonder-working God.

If you've ever been bursting with news about something

God has done in your life—an answer to prayer, a long-awaited blessing, a surprising provision—you didn't want to spill the beans to just anyone. Like Mary, you longed to tell somebody who would get it. A friend who would say, "Praise God!" instead of, "Lucky you."

"The friendship of like-minded women is so important to our emotional and spiritual well-being."

—CHARI

Besides, who else could Mary tell? Her twelve-year-old friends? Her neighbors in Nazareth? "Hey, I just had a visit from an angel, and I'll be giving birth to God's Son."

Right. Not happening. Mary needed Elizabeth.

At that time Mary got ready and hurried... *Luke 1:39*

Clearly, she was keen to hit the road. "Soon afterward" (GNT) and "with little delay" (PHILLIPS), Mary gathered a few travel essentials: perhaps a woven mantle to drape over her linen tunic, a head covering for modesty, and round, flat portions of bread to eat on her journey.[1]

Young as she was, and betrothed besides, she would have needed her parents' permission to travel so far from home and a compelling reason to go. She couldn't inform them Elizabeth was pregnant, or their next question would be "Who told you that?" Our resourceful girl must have offered some credible explanation for wanting to visit her kinswoman, then found a trustworthy family heading south to provide a safe haven for her as she walked among their company.

...to a town in the hill country of Judea,... *Luke 1:39*

Mary likely traveled on foot the whole way. Wheeled carts were a liability across such rough and mountainous terrain, and her family would have been hard pressed to spare a donkey or mule, if they even had one. Horses were a luxury, only for the rich, and camels were used by traders,[2] not by healthy young women like Mary.

The town where Elizabeth and Zechariah lived isn't recorded in Scripture, but according to tradition it was a hilly village west of Jerusalem called Ein Kerem, which means "spring of the vineyard." It's said Mary drank from its cool waters—hence, the famous landmark there known as Mary's Spring.

You can be sure our girl was thirsty, because the traveling distance between Mary's Galilean town of Nazareth and Elizabeth's home outside old Jerusalem is seventy, eighty, or one hundred miles, depending on which path you take and which scholar you ask.

Your mileage may vary, but whatever the distance, it was "a major trip for Mary."[3] Perhaps an unseen host of angels kept watch over her as she hastened across three rock-strewn mountain ranges, a trek of nine or ten days at least.[4]

Joseph was left behind, uninformed. Betrothed couples weren't allowed to speak to each other without someone else present.[5] But she could hardly tell Joseph about her angelic visitor with curious villagers standing around. Nor could she ask a friend of the bridegroom to convey the message, the usual way betrothed couples exchanged information.[6]

Darker concerns loomed on the horizon. An unmarried woman who became pregnant could be dishonored and disgraced at best or stoned to death at worst.[7] To think of innocent Mary having that threat hanging over her! And still she gave herself to God, holding nothing back.

Could any of us be so courageous? Could we demonstrate such faith?

On her long journey south, Mary considered how to tell Elizabeth the news. "I'm carrying God's baby" might not have gone over well in Zechariah's priestly home. Still, according to the angel, her kinswoman had also experienced God's miraculous touch on her womb: "No one thought she could ever have a baby, but in three months she will have a son."[8] Might Elizabeth understand?

When Mary approached her relative's door, she couldn't have guessed the welcome that awaited her.

> ...where she entered Zechariah's home and greeted Elizabeth. *Luke 1:40*

By the sound of it, Mary breezed right in, unannounced by any servant. Open windows and open doors were the order of the day in Judea. Though Zechariah was the homeowner, Mary naturally called out to the woman of the house. If Zechariah was present, he wasn't talking. I mean really not talking. Gabriel had told the priest he would be "reduced to silence,"[9] and indeed he was.

Mary's greeting must have caught Elizabeth by surprise. Had Mary been wealthy, a swift-footed messenger might have been sent ahead. But she was poor, betrothed to a carpenter, "whose entire net worth could fit into a toolbox."[10]

Her unexpected "Hello!" clearly rocked Elizabeth's world.

> When Elizabeth heard Mary's greeting, the baby leaped in her womb,... *Luke 1:41*

Elizabeth was in her sixth month, so she'd already felt her baby boy move. When a mom-to-be eats something sweet or drinks something cold, an unborn child often responds with a swift kick. But this boy didn't just wiggle his toes. When Elizabeth heard Mary's salutation, baby John "jumped" (ERV), he "stirred" (CJB), he "sprang" (GNV). Truth be told, "the young child in her womb gladded" (WYC).

Oh baby. All that gladness swept through Elizabeth like a rushing wind.

> ...and Elizabeth was filled with the Holy Spirit.
> *Luke 1:41*

Whoosh. Not merely filled, but "full-filled with the Holy Ghost" (WYC). Three decades later the Holy Spirit would descend on believers by the hundreds at Pentecost with "the blowing of a violent wind" and "tongues of fire."[11] Elizabeth led the way. Her son was Spirit-filled too, just as Gabriel had promised: "from the time when he is yet a child in his mother's womb he shall be filled with the Holy Ghost."[12]

Can you fathom the emotions and sensations that must have washed over Elizabeth? An urge to laugh and cry at once, a sense of being flooded with sunlight and fresh air, an overwhelming desire to shout with joy.

> In a loud voice she exclaimed:... *Luke 1:42*

Nothing planned here. Elizabeth simply "blurted out" (CEB) what was on her heart. I picture her standing quite close to Mary, perhaps even grasping her hands. So why lift up her voice "with a loud cry" (ASV)? She couldn't help doing so. This was an inspired utterance. This was the Holy Spirit taking charge. The words came from Elizabeth's mouth, but they were formed and fueled by the Holy Spirit at work in her as she "sang out exuberantly" (MSG).

…"Blessed are you among women,…" *Luke 1:42*

Mary had offered no more than a greeting, yet Elizabeth proclaimed her young kinswoman was blessed of the Lord. Only the Holy Spirit could have revealed such a thing. Just as Gabriel had called Mary highly favored, now Elizabeth declared, "God has blessed you more than any other woman" (NCV).

In those days men were the ones who usually conferred blessings. Yet here we have a woman proclaiming a blessing upon another woman. Wow. Even from the womb, Jesus was changing the culture.

"…and blessed is the child you will bear!"
Luke 1:42

Hold it. How could Elizabeth possibly know Mary was pregnant? The child in Mary's womb was no more than two weeks old. Yet Elizabeth blessed "the fruit of thy womb" (ASV).

"Elizabeth prepared the way even before John did!"
—CHRISTINA

Once again this was a revelation of the Holy Spirit. When these words poured out, Elizabeth was surely as dumbfounded as Mary. I'm convinced Zechariah did indeed lose his hearing when he lost his ability to speak. Otherwise, he would surely have heard this exchange and come running. Instead, this remarkable scene was reserved for Elizabeth and Mary.

Think of it! Two ordinary women—one younger, one older; one from a rural area, one from a Jerusalem neighborhood—bound together by an extraordinary God, empowered by his Holy Spirit. They were forever changed. They were filled with life. Through them, God began the salvation of his people, promised through the ages. Through them, God altered the course of history.[13]

Elizabeth—that is to say, the Holy Spirit—had still more to share with Mary.

"But why am I so favored,..." *Luke 1:43*

"Why is God so kind to me?" (NIrV) Elizabeth wanted to know. "Who am I?" (CJB). A question many of us ask when we're convinced we don't deserve the blessings that land in our laps. "Why me, Lord?" we whisper.

God's Word offers the answer: "because of his great love,"[14] because "his compassions never fail,"[15] because God is the one true Source of love and mercy. That's why he blesses us.

Elizabeth was the one favored that day in Ein Kerem when her kinswoman appeared at her door bearing a gift in her womb.

"...that the mother of my Lord should come to me?"
Luke 1:43

Wait a minute, Elizabeth. Not *the* Lord, but *your* Lord? Yes. Elizabeth just made her confession of faith, and Jesus wasn't even born yet. Thirty years would come and go before he would be tempted by Satan in the wilderness, start preaching about repentance, then call his first disciples. Even so, Elizabeth proclaimed him Lord while he was still being formed in his mother's womb.

My mind is blown.

This wasn't Elizabeth taking a leap of faith on her own. This was the Holy Spirit moving inside her as surely as the babe was leaping in her womb.

When you hear a teacher, a pastor, or a speaker utter a statement that rings so true it can only be God, then believe me, *it can only be God.* No man or woman is wise enough, educated enough, or clever enough to understand and communicate the deep truths of God's Word on his or her own. It's entirely a work of the Holy Spirit, and all the applause, all the praise must go to him.

Next Elizabeth revealed something her kinswoman could not see for herself.

> "As soon as the sound of your greeting reached
> my ears, the baby in my womb leaped for joy."
> *Luke 1:44*

The biblical narrator told us the same thing three verses ago. Now it was Mary's turn to hear this astounding news from Elizabeth. "Listen! When I heard your greeting, the baby inside me moved because he was glad" (WE).

Except for some queasiness in the morning or tiredness in the afternoon, Mary may not have noticed any real signs of her pregnancy yet. Elizabeth's words to Mary, then, were a confirmation of God's promise and more powerful than any blood test. Jesus was alive and growing inside her.

You are truly pregnant, Mary. And he is truly God!

What impresses me about Elizabeth was her willingness to defer to her younger relative. Just as her son, John, would be subservient to Jesus—"He must become greater; I must become less"[16]—Elizabeth gladly stepped aside to honor Mary.

This isn't how it usually works with pregnant women. Drop into any Lamaze class, and you'll find a definite pecking order, with the woman closest to term at the top and the newbie decidedly at the bottom. But Elizabeth understood her secondary role and was happy to walk in it, heaping the mother of her Lord with praise.

"There was no competition among these women. It wasn't about them anymore. It was all about the Lord."

—MICHELE

More revelation: the child leaped for *joy,* Elizabeth said. How could she know such a thing? Babies leap without warning, without explanation. But this expectant mom was certain of the reason: *joy,* listed among the fruit of the Holy Spirit,[17] now abundantly pouring forth from Elizabeth.

"Blessed is she who has believed that the Lord would fulfill his promises to her!" *Luke 1:45*

So right. Mary deserved kudos for her faith, which was why Elizabeth commended her. "You believed what the Lord said to you!" Again the Holy Spirit was revealing things Elizabeth could not have known on her own. Mary hadn't told her kinswoman how all this came down. She hadn't described Gabriel's visit, hadn't explained about the hovering of the Holy Spirit. So far, all Mary had said was "Hello." Yet here was Elizabeth, already up to speed, praising Mary's willingness to trust the Lord. "Oh, how happy is the woman who believes in God" (PHILLIPS).

That's the real test of our faith, isn't it? To believe that God's promises are true—not just in theory, but in our everyday lives. To wait with joyful expectancy. To say yes and not be afraid of what others may say about our dependence upon God, about our abundance of joy. If people talk, so what? People always do.

Elizabeth knew a true believer when she saw one. And she wanted nothing more than to serve Mary and keep her by her side.

After such a lyrical welcome, is it any wonder that Mary burst into song? We can hardly imagine Christmas without music: "The First Noel," "O Come, All Ye Faithful," "Silent Night." The list is long, yet the lyrics are embedded deep in our memory banks—well, at least the *first* verses.

Yet more glorious than any familiar carol is the ancient

song born in young Mary's heart. While the exuberant praise of her kinswoman still hung in the air, Mary responded with a song as beautifully rendered as anything in the psalms. It's called "Mary's Hymn of Praise" (NET) or "Mary's Song of Thanks" (NLV), but it's best known as the *Magnificat,* from the Latin translation of Mary's first words, "it magnifies."

And Mary said:... *Luke 1:46*

I know, I know. Not a note has been sung, and already I'm interrupting.

Just as Elizabeth's announcement of Mary's pregnancy came through a revelation of the Holy Spirit, so these magnificent words sprang from a heavenly source. Remember, Mary was neither wellborn nor educated. For her to pour out her praise in such elevated language, it could only be a work of the Holy Spirit within her, as "her noble soul overflows in poetry."[18]

In no way does the Holy Spirit's preeminence diminish Mary's role. On the contrary, it shows us how truly submitted she was to the One whose Seed rested in her womb. She belonged to God completely—mind, body, and soul.

In Mary's words we'll hear echoes of Hannah's song and snippets of David's psalms—a dozen different Old Testament passages in all. As for the tune, she would likely have chosen a familiar chant of the day,[19] even as she sang from her heart.

…"My soul glorifies the Lord…" *Luke 1:46*

Her soul "extols" (AMP); it "exalts" (NASB); it "magnifies" (ESV). Mary's devotion was complete. Her focus, unwavering. She was "bursting with God-news" (MSG). We picture her gaze lifted up, perhaps her hands as well, and her countenance radiant. "My heart is overflowing with praise of my Lord" (PHILLIPS).

> *"Laden with such a burden, Mary was made light and whole by singing."*
>
> —CHRISTINA

Oh, that we might sing along with her and mean every word. Glory, glory, glory to God! Mary was unique among womankind, yet she pointed the way for each of us. *This* is what it means to love and serve God. *This* is what it means to live with a divine purpose. *This* is what it means to put him above everyone and everything. "With all my heart I glorify the Lord!" (CEB).

"…and my spirit rejoices in God my Savior,…"
Luke 1:47

She knew the name of the child inside her: Jesus. "God saves." And like her kinswoman before her, Mary was now confessing her faith in him and in his ability to save her. "My spirit celebrates God, my Liberator!" (VOICE).

No wonder she was "happy" (NLV)! When we lay down the burden of our guilt and shame, when we accept the forgiveness that Jesus offers, when we lift our heads and hearts and embrace the new life he designed for us, our eyes may be flooded with tears, but our faces are filled with joy. Sing out, Mary, and show us how it's done: "In the depths of who I am I rejoice in God my savior" (CEB).

> "…for he has been mindful of the humble state of his servant." *Luke 1:48*

Though Mary insisted, "I am not important" (ERV), she didn't say, "I am humble." To even think that would make a person, well, *not* humble. Counted among the peasants of Nazareth, a town of dubious repute, Mary understood her place. She was fully aware of her "low status" (CEB), her "humble estate" (ESV), her position as God's "lowly servant girl" (NLT).

Even so, God was mindful of her. He'd "taken notice" (CJB); he'd "looked with favor" (CEB); he'd "shown his concern" (NCV). God saw her—I mean really saw her—not with a passing glance, but with a loving gaze as tender as a caress.

God sees you as well, beloved, with compassion in his eyes. No money in the bank? No degree on the wall? No impressive job title printed on a business card? God sees you. No husband to share your bed? No children around your table? No house to call your own? God sees you.

He had a plan for Mary's life, and he has a plan for yours. In our lifetimes we cannot look beyond two or three generations, yet the Holy Spirit was giving Mary a glimpse of eternity.

"From now on all generations will call me blessed,..."
Luke 1:48

As actor Walter Brennan used to say, "No brag. Just fact." Mary wasn't stealing any glory for herself. She was simply acknowledging the truth of God's favor. "All the people who ever shall be will call me the happiest of women!" (PHILLIPS). God's gift to her was so astounding, so undeserved, it would never be forgotten. "From now until the end of time, people will remember how much God blessed me" (ERV).

It's true. We're still talking about Mary. The next generation will do the same, and the next. Mary rightly said, "I'm the most fortunate woman on earth!" (MSG).

Newly pregnant and still unmarried, Mary didn't know what her future would hold, yet she sang with full confidence by the power of the Holy Spirit, "From now on, everyone will consider me highly favored" (CEB). That's trust in action. That's hope with attitude. That's faith with no intention of giving up.

> "...for the Mighty One has done great things for
> me—holy is his name." *Luke 1:49*

In the same sentence Mary quickly returned to glorifying God: "the Powerful One" (ERV), "He Who is almighty" (AMP), and "God All-Powerful" (CEV). If we used such words when we prayed, it might help us grasp whom we're addressing. And who is listening.

Holy, holy, holy. Powerful One. Mighty One.

> "His mercy extends to those who fear him, from
> generation to generation." *Luke 1:50*

This is far more than Mary singing, "He's been good to me." This is an assurance for all generations to come that the Lord will be good to us too, that his "lovingkindness endures" (VOICE). Not because we are good, but because he is goodness itself, offering mercy to those who fear him, revere him, honor him, respect him, worship him—not just then, not just now, but from "age to age" (AMP).

"Mary praised him because she loved him, and because she loved him, she trusted him."

— CATHY

In the verses that follow, Mary tossed in a history lesson, just for good measure. Not only does God extend his mercy into the future; he was also busy in the past—scattering the proud, lifting up the humble, filling the hungry, being merciful to Israel.

> "He has performed mighty deeds with his arm;…"
> *Luke 1:51*

We can almost see the gleam of the armor on our invincible Sovereign God, who "bared his arm and showed his strength" (MSG) and, in doing so, "accomplished mighty deeds" (VOICE).

> "…he has scattered those who are proud in their inmost thoughts." *Luke 1:51*

Look whom God "sent away in disarray" (VOICE): "the high and mighty" (PHILLIPS), "the secretly proud" (CJB), and "those with arrogant thoughts" (CEB). Compared to their hubris, Mary's humility grows even more appealing.

"He has brought down rulers from their thrones…"
Luke 1:52

Surely this was the sort of talk that made Herod the Great nervous. He walked about his palace at night scheming to prevent such a king from ever setting foot in Judea. Yet God "toppled the mighty" (HCSB) and "knocked tyrants off their high horses" (MSG). Tyrants like Herod, whose days were truly numbered.

"…but has lifted up the humble." *Luke 1:52*

This is one of those wonderful *but*s of the Bible. After routing the proud, God "exalted those of low degree" (AMP) and of "humble estate" (ESV). "Those that were not great he has made great" (WE) and "elevated with dignity" (VOICE). Like our Mary.

"He has filled the hungry with good things…"
Luke 1:53

God met the needs of his people—practically, spiritually, financially, emotionally. He made certain "the starving poor sat down to a banquet" (MSG).

"…but has sent the rich away empty." *Luke 1:53*

Another *but,* another comparison. "The callous rich were left out in the cold" (MSG) with "nothing in their hands" (VOICE). God's economy is exactly the opposite of the world's economy. Poor now? Rich for eternity. Rich now? Be generous in your giving. Like the prophet Isaiah before her,[20] Mary urges us to share our food with the hungry, provide the homeless with shelter, clothe the naked. Not just at Christmastime, not just when our giving will earn us a tax deduction, but all through the year.

We hear the Holy Spirit in every syllable of Mary's song. We also recognize that the words Jesus would one day teach his followers—"blessed are the poor in spirit"[21] and "blessed are the meek"[22]—contain echoes of his mother's cries for social justice, balancing the scales between the haves and the have-nots.

"He has helped his servant Israel,…" *Luke 1:54*

Mary knew her people had not been forgotten. Even after the exile in Babylon and four centuries of silence, God still "embraced his chosen child" (MSG).

> "…remembering to be merciful to Abraham and his descendants forever, just as he promised our ancestors." *Luke 1:54–55*

He "piled on the mercies, piled them high" (MSG). God never forgets and never neglects his people. With this child growing inside Mary, the Messiah would not be long in coming. In the meantime, Mary remained in Ein Kerem to be of service to her older kinswoman, who no doubt needed help with her daily tasks as her son's birth drew closer.

> Mary stayed with Elizabeth for about three months and then returned home. *Luke 1:56*

I want more than a sentence. I want a long chapter, if not a whole book, describing how these two women cared for and encouraged each other throughout Elizabeth's last trimester.

"I'm amazed by their spiritual strength and, even more, by their extraordinary unselfishness and their love for each other."

—BRENDA

We can only imagine their daily conversations, filled with the mystery and marvel of what God was doing in their lives. Every detail of their physical and spiritual growth would have been noted with wonder. Minor problems such as indigestion and swollen ankles were surely offset by the delights of motherhood to come.

By the end of those three months, Elizabeth was as round as a full moon. Though Mary might have longed to see Elizabeth's child safely delivered, she could not tarry another day. Mary's baby bump was beginning to show. And Elizabeth's neighbors were beginning to whisper.

Finally, Joseph, her husband-to-be, deserved to know the truth. Following God's certain leading, Mary started home for Nazareth with a child in her womb and a song in her heart.

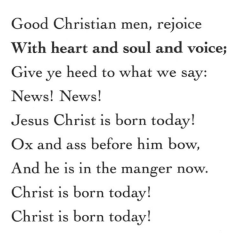

Five

Good Christian men, rejoice
With heart and soul and voice;
Give ye heed to what we say:
News! News!
Jesus Christ is born today!
Ox and ass before him bow,
And he is in the manger now.
Christ is born today!
Christ is born today!

—Translated by John Mason Neale,
"Good Christian Men, Rejoice," 1853

With Heart and Soul and Voice

*O*ne rainy spring I lost my voice for an entire week. Not a word, not even a squeak came out. My husband never confessed as much, but I think he secretly enjoyed having a quiet house. Meanwhile, I discovered how smoothly the world functioned without my constant verbal input. Very humbling. I also learned the value of listening. And praying.

Without uttering a sound, we can still reach out to God.

I suspect that during Mary's visit with Elizabeth, Zechariah had long and meaningful conversations of the heart with his Maker, asking the Lord's forgiveness for doubting his angelic messenger, praising the Lord's mighty name, and seeking the Lord's unfailing counsel.

Surely at the top of Zechariah's prayer list was the safe arrival of his son.

When it was time for Elizabeth to have her baby,...
Luke 1:57

"Elizabeth's full time of being delivered" (DRA) assures us the baby wasn't premature. No hint of a difficult delivery either—a blessing for this older mother. Although Mary had returned to Nazareth, Elizabeth wasn't alone when the time came. God was laboring with her, giving her much-needed strength and courage, just as the psalmist wrote: "You brought me forth from my mother's womb."[1]

A midwife would have been present, wiping Elizabeth's brow and attending to her needs, as well as all the female relatives and friends the house could hold. Childbirth was seldom a private affair. Whether Elizabeth squatted or kneeled or bore down on a horseshoe-shaped birthing stool,[2] those dearest to her would have stood on either side, lifting her up when necessary and offering constant words of encouragement.

There is nothing romantic about the birthing process. Blood, sweat, tears, and all the rest. It's a messy business. Yet when her travail is over, a mother "forgets the anguish because of her joy that a child is born into the world."[3] I know this is true. I labored twenty-six hours to give birth to our firstborn. When they laid that sweet boy in my arms, I looked up at his father, both of us limp with exhaustion, and said, "Let's do this again!"

Whatever Elizabeth went through in giving birth, she would tell you the reward was worth it all. As for Zechariah, he was waiting outside the house with the men of Ein Kerem when that first sharp cry pierced the air.

...she gave birth to a son. *Luke 1:57*

So much joy captured in a single verse! No need to send out announcements. Word was already beginning to spread.

Her neighbors and relatives heard that the Lord had shown her great mercy,... *Luke 1:58*

Elizabeth's "cousins" (wyc), her "kindred" (ylt), her "extended family" (voice) soon discovered "how wonderfully good the Lord had been to her" (gnt). Those same neighbors who'd once looked on barren Elizabeth with pity now gazed at her with awe, witnessing how God had "magnified his mercy towards her" (asv).

Elizabeth—yes, *that* Elizabeth, that old woman—had given birth to a healthy son.

...and they shared her joy. *Luke 1:58*

Can you visualize the scene? People of all ages crowded into every corner of the house, pouring through the door and leaning through the windows. Whatever the size of Ein Kerem, every living soul surely heard the report of this miraculous birth and made tracks for Zechariah's house.

A son at last. A *son*. Even typing the words brings tears to my eyes. To wait so long and not lose hope! Elizabeth finally held in her arms absolute proof of God's love for her. No more barrenness, no more sorrow, no more shame.

"Elizabeth had to wait a long time to see the goodness of God revealed, yet she was faithful, humble, and grateful."
—ALINA

We too can touch and experience living proof of God's love with his printed Word in our hands and the Holy Spirit in our hearts. In Christ our barren lives become rich and full, our sorrows grow dim in the light of his promises, and the shame of our sin is banished forever. An even greater miracle than the birth of a child. An even greater cause for joy.

> On the eighth day they came to circumcise the
> child,... *Luke 1:59*

According to the Law of Moses, every male infant was to be circumcised when he was eight days old as a sign of God's covenant with his people.[4] Once more Elizabeth's neighbors and kinsfolk were on hand for "the child's *b'rit-milah*" (CJB). We can see Elizabeth holding out her baby boy, proud yet understandably anxious when the child's tender foreskin was cut away. *Ouch.* How quickly she must have wrapped him in linen cloths, taking care not to hurt him further. Perhaps she smoothed her cheek against his downy head or sang softly to quiet him.

The time had come to name the boy, so her close relatives took it upon themselves to speak for the head of the household, who still had no voice.

> …and they were going to name him after his father Zechariah,… *Luke 1:59*

Interesting. We don't see this as standard procedure in Scripture. In fact, rarely did a son receive his father's name.[5] For example, not one of Jacob's twelve sons is named Jacob. Nor is it a common practice among Jewish people today. "Many Jews still view it as strange and somewhat arrogant for a father to name a child after himself."[6]

Whether the relatives who shared Elizabeth's joy wanted also to share in the naming process or were simply "becoming meddlesome,"[7] she wasn't having it.

> …but his mother spoke up and said, "No! He is to be called John." *Luke 1:60*

I love this. However wiped out she might have been after a week of sleepless nights spent caring for her son, Elizabeth "intervened" (MSG) with gusto. "Oh, no!" (PHILLIPS) she told them. "Absolutely not!" (GOD'S WORD). That's our role model: standing strong, honoring God. "He shall be called John" (RSV), she informed the crowd.

Her relatives and friends weren't convinced her choice was a sound one.

> They said to her, "There is no one among your relatives who has that name." *Luke 1:61*

Was this a rebuke? Or a reminder? "No one in your family has ever been named John" (CEV), they told her. Since choosing a name outside of the family network was highly suspicious,[8] they might have feared Zechariah would not be seen as the boy's father and wanted to quell any rumors before they started.

When Elizabeth didn't offer another name, her relatives turned to Zechariah.

> Then they made signs to his father, to find out what he would like to name the child. *Luke 1:62*

Hmm. Zechariah was the one who couldn't speak, yet they used "gestures" (NLT) to communicate with him and talked "with their hands" (NLV). Now I'm even more convinced—and so are many scholars—that Zechariah was deaf as well as mute. "It is plain that he lost his hearing as well as his speech, for his friends made signs to him."[9]

If they sought to "find out what he wanted to name his son" (CEV) because Elizabeth's opinion was not sufficient, Zechariah begged to differ.

> He asked for a writing tablet,... *Luke 1:63*

Her husband "motioned" (CJB) for "something to write on" (ERV). Picture a common wooden board with a thin coating of wax, then for writing, a sharp instrument made of gold, silver, brass, iron, copper, ivory, or bone. The opposite end—which was smooth, flat, and circular—served as an eraser so the waxed surface could be used again.[10] Rather sticky on a hot day, but it worked for Zechariah.

> ...and to everyone's astonishment he wrote, "His name is John." *Luke 1:63*

That was the last thing these relatives expected. "How surprised they all were!" (GNT). What happened next gave them even more reason to be "amazed" (NIrV).

Immediately his mouth was opened and his tongue
set free,... *Luke 1:64*

Forget the writing tablet. Zechariah's "power of speech suddenly came back" (PHILLIPS), and his tongue was "loosed" (ASV).
After nine long months that divine restriction was lifted at the
moment of Zechariah's act of obedience. But he didn't stop
there. Zechariah did what came naturally. And supernaturally.

...and he began to speak, praising God. *Luke 1:64*

He didn't ask God why he'd been silenced, nor did he be-
moan the many conversations he'd missed. Instead, Zechariah
"shouted out praises to God" (VOICE).

Elizabeth praised God. Mary praised God. When Zechariah's mouth was opened, he praised God. I'm seeing a pattern
here. You too? Open mouth, praise God. At my house it's more
like open mouth, insert foot. Or open mouth, whine. That's
why I've memorized the following verse and made it my first-
thing-in-the-morning prayer: "Open my lips, Lord, and my
mouth will declare your praise."[11]

David wrote those words after he committed adultery with
Bathsheba. His pride was trampled, and his spirit was humbled,
yet he knew the way out: praising God. That's our way out too.

Out of sin, out of misery, out of fear. When we start praising God for all the great things he has done, there's little time left for whining or worrying. "How good it is to sing praises to our God, how pleasant and fitting to praise him!"[12]

"Instead of complaining, begging, and arguing, I'm praising God!"

—LISA

Elizabeth's delivery of a son and the return of Zechariah's voice were front-page news across the region. Miracle upon miracle.

> All the neighbors were filled with awe, and throughout the hill country of Judea people were talking about all these things. *Luke 1:65*

This is how God works: a blessing for one is a blessing for all, and the end result is a greater focus on him. When we experience his grace, we're compelled to tell others so they may praise the Lord with us. In doing so, their faith is bolstered, knowing that God is real, God is powerful, God is sovereign, and God is moving. Once "a deep, reverential fear settled over the neighborhood" (MSG), the people of Judea "talked about nothing else" (MSG).

Everyone who heard this wondered about it,...
Luke 1:66

They "reflected on these events" (NLT) and "kept *these things* in their hearts" (LEB). They pondered them, considered them, weighed them.

...asking, "What then is this child going to be?"
Luke 1:66

Parents routinely ask such questions. But in the suburbs of Jerusalem, everybody wondered aloud about John. "Whatever will this little boy be then?" (AMP). With all the miracles surrounding his conception and birth, clearly something was special about the lad.

For the Lord's hand was with him. *Luke 1:66*

Ah. No wonder John was the talk of the town. "The Lord's hand" means an "empowering presence."[13] After Zechariah's encounter with an angel, Elizabeth's miraculous conception, and her joyful delivery of baby John, people could see "the Lord's blessing was plainly upon him" (PHILLIPS), both "protecting and aiding him" (AMP).

Did this mean John's life was one of ease with God at the helm? Not for a moment. We can be sure he still fell and skinned his knees, got into childish mischief, and was disciplined by his father. As old as his parents were, John might have been orphaned at a young age—tragic to think about, yet almost a certainty. And his story abruptly ends with his brutal beheading ordered by Herod.[14]

No, John did not have an easy life. Even so, he was God's man, doing God's will, honoring God's name. In the song that burst from Zechariah's lips, we catch a glimpse of the message John would one day proclaim.

> His father Zechariah was filled with the Holy Spirit
> and prophesied:... *Luke 1:67*

Zechariah was a priest, not a prophet—until now. Just as Elizabeth was filled and then their son was filled, Zechariah was filled to the brim with the Spirit of the Lord so he might utter "a prophetic blessing" (VOICE) for the sake of God's people.

Like Mary's *Magnificat*, Zechariah's canticle also has a name—*Benedictus*—from the first word in Latin, meaning "Blessed."[15] Words flowed from Zechariah like living water, refreshing all who heard them.

…"Praise be to the Lord, the God of Israel, because he has come to his people and redeemed them." *Luke 1:68*

Zechariah knew the Lord not only watched and listened; he also "turned his face towards his people and has set them free!" (PHILLIPS).

"He has raised up a horn of salvation for us in the house of his servant David…" *Luke 1:69*

Zechariah wasn't talking about his son, John. He was talking about Jesus, *who was not even born yet.* A horn calls to mind "the great strength of the horned animals of the Near East,"[16] an image that would have quickened their hearts. A "mighty Deliverer" (CJB). A "powerful Savior" (ERV). Yes, please.

"…(as he said through his holy prophets of long ago),…" *Luke 1:70*

"Long ago" is right. "Since the world began" (GNV), indeed "from the very beginning" (CJB), all of creation had waited to be rescued.

"…salvation from our enemies and from the hand of all who hate us—…" *Luke 1:71*

The people of Israel who'd been persecuted for their faith in God had experienced that hatred and longed for the coming Messiah.

"...to show mercy to our ancestors and to remember his holy covenant,..." *Luke 1:72*

Grace is what this Savior would bring. "Mercy *and* compassion *and* kindness" (AMP). Just the opposite of what God's enemies dished out. Furthermore, God would remember his "holy promise" (NLV) to his people.

"...the oath he swore to our father Abraham:..."
Luke 1:73

We have to stretch all the way back to Genesis for that "solemn pledge" (CEB). Two thousand years before Christ—give or take a century—God made a covenant with his people.

"...to rescue us from the hand of our enemies, and to enable us to serve him without fear..." *Luke 1:74*

Zechariah told his neighbors they could serve God "fearlessly" (AMP) and "unafraid" (PHILLIPS). How often I've consoled myself with this reminder from David: "in God I trust and am not afraid. What can man do to me?"[17] The quick answer? Nothing that matters. Not in the long haul.

> "…in holiness and righteousness before him all our days." *Luke 1:75*

We don't generally use such elevated, poetic language. Probably wasn't Zechariah's usual style either. In layman's terms we are made holy and right with God forever.

> "And you, my child, will be called a prophet of the Most High; for you will go on before the Lord to prepare the way for him,…" *Luke 1:76*

We can imagine Zechariah smiling at Elizabeth as he bent over their son, then lifted him as high as his arthritic arms would allow, stretching heavenward as he prophesied, "You will go ahead of the Lord to make his way ready" (WE).

Thirty years later when John was baptizing people in the Jordan River, anticipating the Lord's arrival on the scene, the older residents of Judea must have nodded to one another. *We remember his father's prophecy. Weren't we there? Didn't we hear it for ourselves? Didn't we see the maternal pride that shone in Elizabeth's eyes?*

Zechariah's vision of his son's future ministry was crystal clear.

> "...to give his people the knowledge of salvation
> through the forgiveness of their sins,..." *Luke 1:77*

It was one thing to have sins paid for by an animal sacrificed on an altar. It was something else to proclaim that "deliverance comes by having sins forgiven" (CJB) through a *man,* the Messiah soon to be born.

> "...because of the tender mercy of our God, by
> which the rising sun will come to us from heaven..."
> *Luke 1:78*

I'm thinking how beautiful these words must have sounded when sung. Even if Zechariah wasn't gifted musically, lyrics like "a Light from on high will dawn upon us" (AMP) and "a new day from heaven will shine on us" (ERV) would still shimmer in the air.

> "...to shine on those living in darkness and in the
> shadow of death, to guide our feet into the path of
> peace." *Luke 1:79*

At least in this alto's heart, Zechariah's moving canticle ends with a threefold amen. From darkness to light. *Amen.* From death to life. *Amen.* From conflict to peace. *Amen.*

Elizabeth could not have known a more joy-filled moment. A son safely tucked in her arms. A husband restored to health and rejoicing in God's provision. And a kinswoman in Nazareth carrying the Savior of the world in her womb.

The best stories end on a happy note, and Elizabeth's is no exception. Our sister served the Lord well and blessed his holy name. "Elizabeth could have faced her old age with a sense of failure and waning faith, but her vibrancy of spirit serves as a reminder that God watches over every woman with loving care."[18]

When the Holy Spirit filled Elizabeth, he changed her forever.

If we want to be changed, if we want our lives to be different, if we want to be as faithful as Elizabeth, we won't get there by trying harder or being better or doing more. Instead we must open our hearts and minds to the guidance of the Holy Spirit and trust God to do a mighty work in us, just as he did in Elizabeth.

"We forget that they were just like us and that the things God did in their lives can be done in our lives."

—CANDY

Jesus said of her son, "Truly I tell you, among those born of women there has not risen anyone greater than John the Baptist."[19] A fitting legacy for a woman who lived at full tilt for God.

Now that we have John happily nestled against his mother's breast, you must be wondering about our Mary, who left Elizabeth's house three months pregnant and headed for Nazareth. It can't have been long before her condition became abundantly clear. Let's find out how Mary's husband-to-be, Joseph, handled the news.

> This is how the birth of Jesus the Messiah came about:... *Matthew 1:18*

The opening line rings with anticipation: "So here, *finally,* is the story of the birth of Jesus the Anointed" (VOICE). It's a remarkable account, one we're eager to hear again each December. Yet this gospel writer succeeded in doing what few modern novelists can manage. He summarized the main characters and their plight in a single sentence.

> ...His mother Mary was pledged to be married to Joseph, but before they came together, she was found to be pregnant through the Holy Spirit. *Matthew 1:18*

Reads like a movie trailer, doesn't it? Piquing our curiosity, reeling us in. Until the final phrase this could describe any couple who conceived a child well before their wedding day. But only one woman in history could claim she was "going to have a baby by God's Holy Spirit" (CEV).

Since Mary was *found* to be pregnant, she must not have confessed it verbally. Instead, her changing figure no doubt gave her away. Joseph learned the truth "when it became unmistakable, not when she told him."[20] We can't be certain when this discovery happened, nor is there any record of her family's reaction. Dismay, disappointment, even anger would have been a natural response. In the movie *The Nativity Story,* the actress portraying Mary tells her parents, "I have broken no vow," to which her father retorts, "You have broken every vow, Mary."[21]

Because we know the happy ending, we often forget the harrowing beginning. Mary would have been shunned in her small village. Every door would have been closed to her; every friend would have deserted her. When Mary said yes to God, "the first thing she sacrificed was her reputation."[22] In the same way that Elizabeth's neighbors shook their heads over her barren state when the older woman passed by, so the pious citizens of Nazareth must have gossiped about Mary when she returned home pregnant.

Shame on Elizabeth—a husband but no baby.

Shame on Mary—a baby but no husband.

Her betrothal only complicated matters. Either the unborn child was Joseph's, which marked them both as guilty of sexual immorality, or the child belonged to another man, which meant Mary was an adulteress. The punishment for such a heinous crime was swift and cruel. In Egypt, an adulteress had her nose cut off; in Persia, her nose and ears; in Judea, "the punishment was death by stoning."[23]

Oh my, oh my.

Everything depended on the husband's testimony. He alone could claim her as his wife or charge her with adultery.

> Because Joseph her husband was faithful to the law,...
> *Matthew 1:19*

Much like Zechariah, Joseph is described as "righteous" (ASV), "noble" (MSG), and "godly" (NIrV). A lesser man might have started looking for a few sharp stones, but not this man.

> ...and yet did not want to expose her to public disgrace,... *Matthew 1:19*

Joseph was faithful to the letter of the law, but he was also faithful to the *spirit* of the law. He was grace giving. He was loving. He was merciful. Would God the Father entrust the upbringing of his Son to anyone else? The Lord made certain that Mary was betrothed to a man who was "mild, amiable, and tender."[24] A man like Joseph of Nazareth.

Still, there was the matter of this child growing inside Mary. Joseph could not look away, could not ignore the proof of her infidelity. What a conundrum! Because of his tender affection for her, Joseph refused to "humiliate her" (CEB) and "have her put to open shame" (KNOX). There would be no complaint filed with the magistrate, no public charge of adultery, no trial.[25] But Joseph couldn't wed Mary without incriminating himself.

Even knowing how this ends, I'm biting my lip.

> …he had in mind to divorce her quietly.
> *Matthew 1:19*

Rather than tell anyone, Joseph "resolved" (ESV) what must be done. Since "infidelity during betrothal made divorce almost obligatory,"[26] our law-abiding Joseph had no choice but to break off their engagement. As a kindness to his bride, he would do so "privately" (NET) and "without specifying the cause."[27] That way he could maintain his personal righteousness yet spare Mary from possible death.[28]

Alas, here's what that plan would have meant for Mary. No

husband, ever. No father for her child. Living with family members to the end of her days. Bringing a permanent sense of dishonor to the household. Enduring a shame she did not deserve.

God, of course, had a better plan.

> But... *Matthew 1:20*

There it is again, one of my favorite words in the Bible, especially when it signals something is about to change for the better.

> ...after he had considered this,... *Matthew 1:20*

Joseph did not act in haste. He thought things through. Prayed things through. He "contemplated" (NET); he "pondered" (MOUNCE). When at last Joseph decided to sleep on it, "God graciously directed him what to do."[29]

> ...an angel of the Lord appeared to him in a dream... *Matthew 1:20*

This isn't Gabriel. This is an angel of the Lord, "a manifestation of Yahweh,"[30] visiting Joseph in his sleep. Since the time of the patriarchs, the Lord had spoken to his people through dreams, as he did here.

> …and said, "Joseph son of David,…"
> *Matthew 1:20*

Adding the family name let Joseph know the angel had come to the right dreamer. It wasn't a conversation, though. The angel did all the talking.

> "…do not be afraid to take Mary home as your
> wife,…" *Matthew 1:20*

Usually when an angel says "fear not" (KJV), he is cautioning the hearer not to be afraid of him. In this case the angel was telling Joseph not to be afraid of doing right by Mary. "Do not fear that she will be unworthy of you, or will disgrace you"[31] was the gist of it. The angel's nudge was gentle but firm. "Go ahead and marry her" (CEV).

Despite appearances, Mary had remained virtuous and pure, while taking good care of herself and her baby. If she was in her fifth month of pregnancy, then her growing child was nearly ten inches long with a soft downy covering on his body.[32] Fully human and fully God.

> "…because what is conceived in her is from the Holy
> Spirit." *Matthew 1:20*

Had Mary already told Joseph this wondrous truth, making the angel's words mere confirmation? Or was Joseph hearing this astounding news for the first time? Either way, he might have fainted had he been awake. "Mary's pregnancy is Spirit-conceived" (MSG)? *Oh baby.*

> "She will give birth to a son, and you are to give him
> the name Jesus,…" *Matthew 1:21*

Angels really go at a clip, don't they? Spilling out one life-changing fact after another.

When this son was born, Joseph was to name him Jesus, "Savior" (AMP). Yet some months earlier Gabriel had told Mary, "You are to call him Jesus."[33] So who was meant to do the naming? Both of them, just as modern parents do. Zechariah and Elizabeth each spoke John's name in turn. Imagine the delight for Mary and Joseph when they confessed to each other that an angel had provided the perfect name.

> "…because he will save his people from their sins."
> *Matthew 1:21*

The gospel, preached to Joseph in the middle of the night. The good news, preached to everyone who reads God's Word and discovers the Lord has brought his people "rescue, salvation, deliverance" (OJB).

"I am amazed at how much God loves us and desires to bring us into a relationship with him no matter what it takes."

—PHYLLIS

Love. That's what is written across our hearts and throughout this story. Because of love, God trusted a brave young woman and an honest, hardworking carpenter with the precious gift of his Son.

> All this took place to fulfill what the Lord had said through the prophet:... *Matthew 1:22*

This reminder was not spoken aloud to Joseph, but surely the following prophecy came to mind—if not that night, then soon thereafter. The gospel writer is about to quote Isaiah 7:14, written more than seven hundred years before the birth of Jesus.[34] At long last, in God's perfect timing, these prophetic words from centuries ago were bearing fruit.

"The virgin will conceive and give birth to a son, and they will call him Immanuel" (which means "God with us"). *Matthew 1:23*

A virgin? Check. A conception? Done. A son? Guaranteed. His name? Already decided. "God saves." "God with us." "Jesus."

When Joseph woke up,... *Matthew 1:24*

Wake up, Joseph! Wake up to the truth, to the light, to a whole new world. As he "arose from his sleep" (ASV), he didn't bother with breakfast or spend an hour in the shower. Joseph was a man on a mission from God.

...he did what the angel of the Lord had commanded him... *Matthew 1:24*

Joseph was a perfect match for Mary. He "did as the messenger of the Lord directed him" (YLT), just as she had accepted what the Lord required of her. Could a man ask for any greater blessing than to be married to the woman God chose to bear his Son?

...and took Mary home as his wife. *Matthew 1:24*

They were "soon married" (CEV). I'm picturing a fairly low-key wedding—no bridesmaids, a small cake—before Joseph "brought her into his home" (VOICE). Some of the wedding guests no doubt muttered about Joseph making an honest woman of Mary. Little did they know how innocently these two would live as husband and wife.

> But he did not consummate their marriage until she gave birth to a son. *Matthew 1:25*

They "had no union" (AMP), no "marital relations" (GOD'S WORD). Yes, we understand.

Joseph certainly didn't mean to punish her. It's inconsistent with the man we've seen thus far. Joseph may simply have intended to protect his pregnant wife. Perhaps he thought of Isaiah's prophecy and realized Mary needed to remain a virgin until Jesus was born. Or maybe he thought her too sacred to be touched and did not want to risk interfering with God's plan. In any case, Joseph showed great restraint, taking this young bride into his home and onto his pallet, yet "he knew her not" (DRA).

Here's something that often goes unnoticed: Joseph doesn't say a word in Scripture. He wasn't unable to speak, as Zechariah was. But whatever Joseph said, his words came and went unrecorded.

And though he raised Jesus, Joseph was clearly not his father. When Jesus began his public ministry at age thirty, his genealogy states, "He was the son, so it was thought, of Joseph."[35] *So it was thought.* Joseph knew better. Jesus didn't have one drop of his blood. Even so, Joseph redeemed the young woman whom God had chosen for him and ignored the gossip that chased after them like scrappy dogs nipping at their heels.

Elizabeth and Zechariah had risen above the rumors, their eyes fixed on bringing a fine son into the world. Now it was Mary and Joseph's turn to do the same. To look to God for strength and to lean on each other through the difficult days ahead.

"I am so encouraged by the faith that Elizabeth and Mary had. It takes an open heart and a willing spirit to follow God no matter what people might say."
—TRACY

Mary surely watched the phases of the moon and counted the months as they passed. *Six. Seven. Eight.* Perhaps her own birthday came and went during her pregnancy. Did her parents forgive her? believe her? support her? Or did she and Joseph truly go it alone? Though the Bible doesn't tell us, my hope is that grace prevailed, at least within their families.

We can picture her walking through the olive groves around Nazareth with one hand resting on her belly, instinctively protecting her son. Scolding him when he kicked too hard, whispering endearments when she felt him gently turning inside her. Praying she would be ready. Praying all would go well.

Soon, dear one. Soon.

Six

How silently, how silently
The wondrous gift is given!
So God imparts to human hearts
The blessings of his heaven.
No ear may hear his coming,
But in this world of sin,
Where meek souls will receive him still,
The dear Christ enters in.

—Phillips Brooks, "O Little
Town of Bethlehem," 1867

The Wondrous Gift
Is Given

*I*t was time.

All across Judea people went about their business, trading their goods and tending their flocks, unaware, unprepared. But Mary, Joseph, and all of heaven knew.

He is coming.

Centuries earlier the prophet Micah foretold the place where Jesus would be born: "But you, Bethlehem Ephrathah, though you are small among the clans of Judah, out of you will come for me one who will be ruler over Israel, whose origins are from of old, from ancient times."[1] This meant God had to transport Mary from Nazareth to Bethlehem before she gave birth. As Gabriel pointed out, "God can do anything!"[2] Why not a census?

> In those days Caesar Augustus issued a decree that a
> census should be taken of the entire Roman world.
> *Luke 2:1*

We do a US census every decade, as our Constitution requires. In Mary's day the Roman emperor was the one who proclaimed when "all the world should be enrolled" (ASV), making certain every citizen's name was "listed in record books" (CEV).

> (This was the first census that took place while
> Quirinius was governor of Syria.) *Luke 2:2*

A historical aside meant to establish the date. Caesar needed to know precisely how many people he'd conquered so he could tax them properly. He also wanted to remind them who was in charge. Oh, the foolishness of humankind, considering "the cattle on a thousand hills"[3] belong to the Lord, and he alone is "God over all the kingdoms of the earth."[4] Still, the people of Judea were wary of Rome and its powerful leaders, so they did what was required of them.

> And everyone went to their own town to register.
> *Luke 2:3*

Not necessarily to where they had been born but to "the village of their ancestral origin."[5] By matching people with their homelands, Caesar could determine the strength of each tribe. From his viewpoint in Rome, this exercise was purely political.

From God's viewpoint in heaven, it was purely spiritual. Mary had to be moved.

> So Joseph also went up from the town of Nazareth in Galilee to Judea,... *Luke 2:4*

Mary now faced the same journey she'd taken many months earlier to see Elizabeth, just after the Christ child was conceived. This time Mary would travel even farther, to a town five or six miles south of Jerusalem.

> ...to Bethlehem the town of David, because he belonged to the house and line of David. *Luke 2:4*

We're reminded why Jesus is called the Son of David. His earthly father, Joseph, was in the lineage of that famous king and went to Bethlehem for the census "because he was from David's family" (CEV).

Though Bethlehem was much larger than Nazareth, it still housed fewer than a thousand residents.[6] Considering David's eight wives, numerous concubines, and all their offspring, this little town of Bethlehem would have been bursting at the seams with David's descendants by the time Joseph and his pregnant wife arrived.

He went there to register with Mary, who was
pledged to be married to him... *Luke 2:5*

Wait. Weren't they married by now? They were, but words
such as "betrothed" (ASV) and "promised" (GOD'S WORD) were
still used because they'd "not yet consummated the marriage."[7] Sure, they'd tied the knot, but Mary remained chaste,
innocent.

...and was expecting a child. *Luke 2:5*

The miracle continued: a virgin yet "great with child" (ASV).
We're left to wonder how this newlywed couple spent their first
few months together. Fending off the Galilean gossips? Praying
for God's protection? Learning to be patient with each other,
like most married couples? What a unique bond they must
have had—both of them visited by an angel, both entrusted
with raising the Messiah—while all during those nine months,
"divinity resided within her womb."[8]

*"Faithful girl. Faithful God. What a miracle
to use a young woman who could be like any
of us."*

—SHARI

As for their journey to Bethlehem, no details are given. Honest, not a word. But common sense, historical records, and a map should give us some clues.

Two routes were the most likely. One forded the Jordan River, traveled south along the eastern shore for sixty miles, then crossed the river again near Jericho and climbed west to Bethlehem.[9] This way they would have avoided the land of the Samaritans—a people considered unclean, even heretical by the Jews[10]—and traveled a more level route through the river plain. But it would have added another twenty or thirty miles to their journey, requiring a minimum of two extra days.[11]

The other route was far more direct, taking them due south from Nazareth through the Jezreel Valley and along the Way of the Patriarchs.[12] Not only was this route shorter; it also passed by many wells, providing much-needed water. Whichever path they chose, they likely journeyed with a caravan of other travelers bound for Bethlehem, seeking safety in numbers for their trek of eight to ten days along roads where swindlers and thieves looked for easy prey.[13]

We can't be certain how close to term Mary was, but definitely "in the later stages of her pregnancy" (PHILLIPS). Tradition and Hollywood often show her reaching the edge of town at the first contraction, but that's not found in Scripture. She and

Joseph may have been in Bethlehem for some time before she went into labor. With a sigh of relief, we can probably let go of the image of an about-to-give-birth Mary being jostled on the back of a donkey.

Even so, she didn't have long to wait. Joseph and Mary were still in Bethlehem, the streets and houses crowded with visitors, when her pregnant days were over.

> While they were there, the time came for the baby
> to be born,... *Luke 2:6*

Like John before him, Jesus didn't come prematurely but arrived when "the days were fulfilled" (ASV), and "she came to the end of her time" (PHILLIPS) at the exact moment God had ordained.

> ...and she gave birth to her firstborn, a son.
> *Luke 2:7*

Forgive me, Lord, but *that's it*? Your holy Son, born in a single verse?

Yes.

Whether she labored three hours or thirty, whether a midwife was present or Joseph alone assisted in the delivery process, Mary gave birth to a son. We have no birthweight, no length, no Apgar score. Were his extremities pink? Was his pulse rate over one hundred? Did he have a strong, lusty cry?

Here's what matters most: the prophecies had all come true, the miracle was complete, and the Savior rested in Mary's embrace. This child of the Holy Spirit was her child too, with ten tiny fingers and ten tiny toes, with olive skin and a dark whorl of hair. "The Word became flesh and made his dwelling among us."[14] On that sacred day God became more than a pillar of cloud or a pillar of fire.[15] He became flesh and blood and bone. He became one of us.

"When it really sinks in—all that Jesus is, starting with that simple birth—the true meaning of Christmas is almost too much for my human heart, mind, and soul to comprehend."

—NICOLE

Even if her son did arrive in busy Bethlehem rather than in her hometown of Nazareth, Mary was ready to step into her maternal role. In the ancient Near East, that meant his body was washed in water, rubbed in salt mixed with olive oil to cleanse the skin, then dressed in standard attire for a newborn: swaddling clothes.[16]

She wrapped him in cloths… *Luke 2:7*

Picture them as "strips of cloth" (LEB), simple linen bands, wrapped tightly around him like bandages such that "no sign of arms or legs, hands or feet, could be seen."[17] According to the Talmud, this was to straighten the limbs,[18] but every mother knows a newborn simply wants to feel warm and protected.

Now consider this: the first person to hold the newborn Christ was Mary of Nazareth, and the first person to touch the newly risen Christ, however briefly, was Mary of Magdala.[19] God placed himself in a woman's care when he came to earth, then entrusted a woman to announce his resurrection when he came back to life.

When I hear women rail that the Bible is misogynistic, I wonder if we're reading the same book. God loves women, redeems women, empowers women—then and now. On the day we call Christmas, he could have simply arrived on earth, yet he chose to enter through a virgin's womb. On the day we call Easter, he could have appeared first to his beloved disciple, John, yet he chose as his first witness a woman set free from seven demons.[20]

Women are precious to him, beloved. You are precious to him. In the same way, Mary was dear to the One whose Son she held in her arms.

…and placed him in a manger,… *Luke 2:7*

Like Moses, "who was in his infancy cast out in an ark of bulrushes,"[21] the Christ child was laid on "a bed of hay" (CEV) in a trough that held fodder for animals. Before now we weren't told this family was in such a humble setting. How it must have grieved Joseph, a carpenter, not to have a wooden cradle, built with his own tools. Instead, it was "a box where cows feed" (WE). Though it doesn't sound appealing, what it does sound is "safe, sturdy, and raised above the animals' hooves."[22] Some comfort there.

But why were they lodging with livestock rather than with people?

> …because there was no guest room available for them.
> *Luke 2:7*

We're more familiar with the phrase "there was no room for them in the inn" (KJV), which has prompted many a Christmas drama about a modern Mary and Joe pulling into the parking lot of a low-budget motel with a No Vacancy sign blinking on and off, announcing the sorry news.

Our own firstborn son arrived two weeks late on a hot August night while we were living in a small inner-city house with no air conditioning. Still, that minimal amount of discomfort was nothing compared to Mary's first hours as a mother. She was in the sticks, quite literally, in a place that reeked of moldy hay and manure.

Given the circumstances, it's surprising what we *don't* find in this passage. *She whined. She complained. She demanded better accommodations.* Not our Mary. Even after giving birth to the Savior of the world, she didn't insist on special treatment, didn't fuss about there being "no space for them in the living-quarters" (CJB).

So where were they exactly?

Perhaps they'd intended to stay in a large "caravan shelter" (EXB), built for public use so that a traveler and his beast could find lodging.[23] But with the census under way, even the caravan shelters were overflowing, and "there was no room for them in the house for strangers" (WE).

Mary had no choice but to give birth in a place meant for animals. Most likely a stable[24] or beneath a lean-to propped against an opening to one of the limestone caves around Bethlehem.[25] Frankly, it was the last place any woman would want to give birth.

"When Jesus was ready to enter this world, there was no room for him. We weren't preparing for him. Yet he is preparing a place for us."

—SUSAN

Here's the hard truth: when Jesus was born, he was for a brief time homeless.[26] Though he would grow up with four walls around him in Nazareth, he would become homeless again as an adult when his ministry began in earnest: "Foxes have dens and birds have nests, but the Son of Man has no place to lay his head."[27] From beginning to end he was poor, with few material goods to call his own.

The Lord chose to be born into poverty, to identify with the unseen of society—the unkempt, the unpopular, the undernourished. His earthly parents had nothing the world counts as valuable. "Had they been rich, room would have been made for them."[28] Instead, they were poor, yet they made room in their hearts for God.

On that day in Bethlehem, absolute abasement was bathed in breathtaking glory. Born the lowest of the low, the infant Jesus was the highest of the high.

What is God saying to us? The rich cannot depend on their riches. The mature must become like children. Those who are full of themselves must be emptied for their Savior to enter in. It's no accident that when the heavenly host came to earth, they sought the company of shepherds, not kings.

> And there were shepherds living out in the fields
> nearby,... *Luke 2:8*

An obvious and fitting choice. David was a shepherd, Jesus is called our Shepherd,[29] and "we are his people, the sheep of his pasture."[30]

But here's the thing: shepherds were despised. They couldn't keep the ceremonial laws while traveling about the hills, they were often regarded as thieves, and because they were considered unreliable, they were not permitted to give evidence in court.[31]

Yet this was whom God chose for his witnesses and entrusted with his good news. Men of humble means, they too were homeless, living outside "under the open sky" (AMP) near Bethlehem. Even in the winter the animals meant to be used for temple sacrifices were kept out in the fields.[32]

One November morning I looked down on those grazing lands outside Bethlehem, where Ruth gleaned and Boaz redeemed, where a boy named David once tended his father's sheep. A broad hillside with an expansive view, it must have provided an ideal vantage point for these shepherds. At that late hour the fields might have been awash in moonlight as the men pulled their cloaks around them for warmth.

> …keeping watch over their flocks at night. *Luke 2:8*

Since shepherding was done around the clock, the men worked "in shifts" (AMP), some sleeping while others guarded the flocks from robbers and predatory animals.[33] As they peered into the darkness, their ears tuned to the bleating of the sheep, heaven came down to earth.

An angel of the Lord appeared to them,... *Luke 2:9*

The shepherds were surely taken aback, perhaps were even speechless, as this messenger "stood before them" (NASB) either on the ground or poised above it.

...and the glory of the Lord shone around them,...
Luke 2:9

Who could say a word while the "the brightness of the Lord's glory flashed" (CEV) and the "shining-greatness of the Lord" (NLV), blinding in its brilliance, "blazed around them" (PHILLIPS). On that holiest of nights, we can almost hear a clear-voiced tenor singing, "Fall on your knees!" Maybe the shepherds did just that.

...and they were terrified. *Luke 2:9*

If "the fear of the LORD is the beginning of wisdom,"[34] these were the true wise men that night, for the shepherds "were sore afraid" (ASV). The phrase is amplified in the Greek: "they dreaded with great dread" (WYC).

> But the angel said to them, "Do not be afraid."
> *Luke 2:10*

We've heard this before. Four times in our story, God's messenger was quick to say, "Fear not!" (WE), offering encouragement to a frightened soul. God whispers those words to his daughters as well whenever we lose heart or give fear a toehold. "Don't be afraid!" (CEV).

The shepherds were about to discover that God didn't send an angel to destroy them but to bless them.

> "I bring you good news that will cause great joy
> for all the people." *Luke 2:10*

This "wonderful, joyous news" (CEB), these "glad tidings of great joy" (GNV) were meant for "all the people," a phrase in the Greek that "usually refers to 'the whole people of Israel.'"[35] God's people, then and now.

> "Today in the town of David…" *Luke 2:11*

On "this very day" (CJB), as Isaiah had prophesied, a momentous event had taken place "in Bethlehem, the city of David!" (NLT). The shepherds must have looked at one another, mouths agape, leaning on their staffs to keep from fainting. *Here? In our town?*

"…a Savior has been born to you;…" *Luke 2:11*

An infant, and already he was "a Deliverer" (CJB), "a Liberator" (VOICE). Then came the biggest and best news of all. He had not merely come to rescue the Israelites someday as the general of an army or the leader of their nation. Oh no. Far more than that.

"…he is the Messiah, the Lord." *Luke 2:11*

So many names and titles have been given to "the promised Anointed One, the Supreme Authority!" (VOICE). He is worthy of them all. For God's people the wait was finally over. "Long-looked for is come at last."[36]

The angel wasn't finished yet.

"How amazing to have one of the heavenly host come down and proclaim such news!"

—TRACY

"This will be a sign to you:…" *Luke 2:12*

Zechariah, you'll remember, asked for a sign because he wasn't convinced. The shepherds didn't ask for a sign, didn't demand proof, didn't insist on seeing the child. They took the angel at his word. Still, the Lord wanted them to look and see, because he needed them to go and tell. So the angel said, "Let this prove it to you" (PHILLIPS).

> "...You will find a baby wrapped in cloths and lying in a manger." *Luke 2:12*

We've seen countless Christmas cards and tabletop Nativity scenes with Jesus as a "newborn baby" (CEB), dressed in "swaddling-clothes" (KNOX) and "lying in a feeding box" (ERV). But we've had a lifetime to embrace that reality. Think of these men hearing it for the first time! *A manger?*

Before the shepherds had time to wonder or to question or to doubt...oh!

> Suddenly... *Luke 2:13*

God clearly loves to do the unexpected, reinforcing his authority and demonstrating his power. First he sent one angelic messenger. Then "straightway" (GNV), "in a flash" (PHILLIPS), reinforcements arrived.

...a great company of the heavenly host appeared with the angel,... *Luke 2:13*

The hills of Bethlehem were filled with a "vast army" (CJB), a "multitude of heavenly soldiers" (GNV) made up of "thousands of other messengers" (VOICE). Can you see them, beloved? Thousands of angels.

...praising God and saying,... *Luke 2:13*

From the moment of their creation, angels have been "giving thanks to God" (NLV). Now imagine *thousands* of voices honoring him in perfect unison.

But were they actually singing? The Greek word *legontōn* is translated "saying," "speaking," or "talking" but not, alas, "singing." I spent an afternoon studying and Googling and fretting over how "the world in solemn stillness lay to hear the angels sing" if they didn't actually sing but simply spoke their praise.

Then several clues began to fit together. God told Job of a time when "the morning stars sang together and all the angels shouted for joy."[37] Also, *singing, shouting,* and *praising* are often used interchangeably, as in "My lips will shout for joy when I sing praise to you."[38] Most encouraging of all is the command

"Sing for joy, O heavens!"[39] Undeniably, that's the heavenly host singing.

My fears were laid to rest. The shepherds could join in the carol "Angels we have heard on high, sweetly singing o'er the plains," though perhaps they were singing strongly rather than sweetly. Because when the following words poured forth from that "huge angelic choir" (MSG), the sound was surely so powerful, so beautiful, so worshipful, the earth must have trembled beneath the shepherds' feet.

> …"Glory to God in the highest heaven, and on earth peace to those on whom his favor rests."
> *Luke 2:14*

An army bringing news of peace! And not "good will toward men," as we often say, but "peace among people of good will!" (CJB). Peace comes from knowing God. That's why the angels proclaim peace to "God's friends" (KNOX), to "all men and women on earth who please him" (MSG). As Matthew Henry so eloquently put it, "All the good we have, or hope, is owing to God's good-will; and, if we have the comfort of it, he must have the glory of it."[40]

> When the angels had left them and gone into heaven,… *Luke 2:15*

Did they leave as quickly as they had appeared? Or fade out of view as they ascended and "returned to heaven" (CEB)? We know only that the angels "departed" (DRA), leaving the shepherds to find their voices again.

> ...the shepherds said to one another, "Let's go to Bethlehem..." *Luke 2:15*

"As fast as we can" (MSG), they said, prepared to "rush down to Bethlehem right now!" (VOICE). The frightened and faint of heart had now become the fearless, so determined to go that they were willing to leave their sheep.

> "...and see this thing that has happened, which the Lord has told us about." *Luke 2:15*

The shepherds had listened. Now they wanted to see and "experience" (VOICE) this thrilling truth in person.

Get ready, Mary. You're about to have company.

I love when a friend stops by unexpectedly. But a van full of dirty, woolly, sleep-outdoors-in-their-clothes strangers showing up without warning? Mary deserves the Miss Hospitality award.

> So they hurried off and found Mary and Joseph, and the baby, who was lying in the manger. *Luke 2:16*

Again that sense of urgency as "they went running" (ERV) and "came with haste" (DRA). They couldn't abandon their flocks for long. But they had to see the Messiah. If Mary had given birth in someone's house behind closed doors, the shepherds might have had difficulty locating him. But a newborn baby in a feed trough? Surely there was only one of those in Bethlehem that night.

When Mary and Joseph looked up to find shepherds drawing near, they might have had a moment of concern, until the men explained they were sent by an angel. Think of the overwhelming sense of awe and relief that must have swept over this couple. *An angel!* This child truly was God's Son. Furthermore, the Almighty was still involved in their lives, still watching over them, still caring for them.

For Mary's sake and their own, the shepherds didn't overstay their welcome. They looked; they marveled. Then it was time to go.

When they had seen him,... *Luke 2:17*

The "him"—or "it" in some translations—is only implied in the original Greek. They had simply *seen*. Their eyes were opened. They had living proof. "Seeing was believing" (MSG) for these honest men of the hills. "Seeing, they understood" (DRA) and did not hesitate to tell others.

…they spread the word concerning what had been told them about this child,… *Luke 2:17*

The Bible doesn't note how many shepherds "became the first preachers of the gospel,"[41] but you can be sure it was enough. Handpicked by God, "they publicized widely" (WEB) all they'd seen and heard.

"May we be like the shepherds, going about telling all who are willing to listen!"

—TOSIN

The shepherds heard, then saw, and so were ready to tell the world. We, too, usually hear the gospel first, then see it lived out before we can say with all our hearts, "I know that my redeemer lives."[42]

…and all who heard it were amazed at what the shepherds said to them. *Luke 2:18*

No kidding! People were "astounded" (AMP), "surprised" (NLV), and "impressed" (MSG) by their reports. Though the men might have been more at ease on the hills with their sheep than moving among the townsfolk, they had to share the good news.

What about Mary? Did she run around Bethlehem, telling everyone about God's Son? She did not.

> But Mary treasured up all these things and pondered them in her heart. *Luke 2:19*

Mary focused on caring for her baby while she stored all she'd seen and done "like a secret treasure in her heart" (NIrV). Some women like to talk their way through experiences; others prefer the Mary approach: "weighing *and* pondering" (AMP), "mulling them over" (CJB), and "trying to understand them" (ERV).

Sometimes the Lord does such a profound work in us and through us that sharing it with others would sound like bragging. Even if we say, "Look what God has done," others may perceive it as "Look what I've done" or "Look how special I am!"

God, as always, knows best. The shepherds were noisy, yet the mother of Jesus was quiet. Others would take his story far and wide, encircling the earth with his truth. Mary was called to be his mother—no more and no less. To nurture him, to feed and clothe him, to teach him all she knew of his heavenly Father.

As to these things she had treasured up, "holding them dear, deep within herself" (MSG), Gabriel had given her quite a list of attributes for this child, starting with "He will be great and will be called the Son of the Most High."[43] Whenever she held her baby boy, those angelic words surely ran through her mind. He didn't look like a monarch, but one day he would be called "Lord of lords and King of kings."[44] He didn't have the strength to hold up his head, let alone stand on his feet, yet he is the One "who is able to keep you from stumbling and to present you before his glorious presence without fault and with great joy."[45]

"Oh, to be like Mary—quiet, humble, willing, obedient, focused."

—SHERRY

Just as Mary "committed these things to memory" (CEB), we can do the same—not only at Christmastime, but all through the year—thinking about who Jesus is and why he came to earth as a babe wrapped in swaddling clothes.

He came for those he loves.

He came for you.

> The shepherds returned, glorifying and praising God for all the things they had heard and seen, which were just as they had been told. *Luke 2:20*

They didn't abandon their flocks after all. Having proclaimed the good news on their short-term mission trip, they "returned home" (CEB) and "went back to their sheep" (ERV), still praising God and "thanking him for everything" (NCV). Like the woman at the well who met the Christ, then hurried back to her town,[46] the shepherds returned to the place where they were known and there made Christ known.

And what of sweet Mary? Was she praising God too?

Even when a healthy young woman gives birth, she needs time to adjust to being a mother, and her body needs time to recover as well. Perhaps Joseph was able to find more suitable lodging for them in a caravan or cave. Once the shepherds spread the news, you can be sure others sought out this little family, wanting to see if the astounding tale could possibly be true.

Mary would have been the one to usher them into her temporary home and allow them a glimpse of God's Son—sleeping, no doubt, since newborns wake only long enough to eat before drifting off again. Mary would have had many hours to gaze at Jesus, to lightly stroke his cheek, to kiss his tiny fists and wonder what the future might hold.

"This very day in David's town your Savior was born."[47]

Yes, he was. Your Savior and mine. All because one woman said yes to God.

Seven

And our eyes at last shall see him,
Through his own redeeming love;
For that Child so dear and gentle,
Is our Lord in heaven above,
And he leads his children on,
To the place where he is gone.

—CECIL FRANCES ALEXANDER,
"ONCE IN ROYAL DAVID'S CITY," 1849

And Our Eyes at Last
Shall See Him

*T*o us a Child of God was born. To us a Son of God was given. Yet Mary was the one who nursed him at her breast and washed his swaddling clothes and sang him to sleep. She was the one who studied every crease and dimple in his body, who knew the scent of his skin, who recognized the distinct note of his cry.

A new mother does her best to hold the world at bay as she bonds with her child. But Mary didn't have the luxury of time. Even before the shepherds had departed, another group of men were already en route, seeking the Messiah.

Scholars differ on the timing of the wise men's arrival. Was it soon after Christ's birth? months later? two years later? Whenever they appeared, we'll spend a moment with them now and consider what they bring to the story—far more than mere gold, frankincense, and myrrh.

> After Jesus was born in Bethlehem in Judea, during
> the time of King Herod, Magi from the east came to
> Jerusalem... *Matthew 2:1*

Manger scenes generally feature three men dressed in royal garments, perhaps inspired by the Victorian Christmas carol "We Three Kings of Orient Are," though historians of old believed there may have been as many as fourteen Magi. Whatever their number, these men of wealth and influence likely hailed from ancient Persia—modern Iran—traveling due west nearly a thousand miles to Israel, a journey of several months.[1]

Rather than kings, the Bible calls them "a party of astrologers" (PHILLIPS), "a band of scholars" (MSG), or simply "wise men" (CEV). The word *Magi* has the same root as *magic,* though there was nothing dark or sinister about these gentlemen who "studied the stars" (GNT), knowing the One who made them.[2]

Once they reached Jerusalem, the Magi explained to Herod that they'd come on a pilgrimage, seeking the newborn king of the Jews.

> "...We saw his star when it rose and have come to
> worship him." *Matthew 2:2*

While scientists are still sorting out what the Magi might have seen—a comet? a planet? a meteor?—we recognize that

God had clearly arranged the ideal sign for a group of stargazers, "a candle set up on purpose to guide them to Christ."[3] The One who'd filled the sky with thousands of angels could surely place a supernaturally bright star in the heavens to announce his Son's birth.

> When King Herod heard this he was disturbed, and all Jerusalem with him. *Matthew 2:3*

The birth of a king is never good news when you're the one in charge. Herod was "alarmed" (NET), even "terrified" (MSG). He called for the chief priests and asked them where this king was to be born. "In Bethlehem," they told him, quoting the prophet Micah: "for out of you will come a ruler who will shepherd my people Israel."[4]

Uh-oh.

Herod met with the Magi secretly, found out the exact time the star had first appeared, then sent the travelers ahead to Bethlehem, urging them to search for the child and report back so he could worship the boy too. We know better. A man evil enough to execute his wife and two sons would not bow his knee to a newborn.

The Magi went on their way, following the star until it stopped. Now *that* is a miracle. All stars appear to move, because the earth is turning on its axis. But this star came to a halt "above the place where the little child lay."[5] No wonder the Magi were filled with "exceeding great joy"![6]

> On coming to the house, they saw the child with his mother Mary,... *Matthew 2:11*

Some time had indeed passed, then, because the Magi came not to a stable or a lean-to or a cave but to a true house, as the Greek word *oikian* assures us. And Jesus was no longer a newborn, a *brephos,* but a *paidion,* which means "a child under training," old enough to respond to discipline and instruction.

Imagine our small-town girl gazing up at these richly dressed Magi bearing gifts fit for a king. When the shepherds had come speaking of angels, Mary had known her child was indeed the Son of God. Now powerful scholars had journeyed a vast distance in search of a king, again confirming what Gabriel had once told her: "The Lord God will give him the throne of his father David."[7]

The meaning behind these visits could not be clearer: Jesus came for the whole world. Near and far, poor and wealthy, Jew and Gentile, servant and king. The Magi had come, not to venerate Mary, but to pay homage to her son.

> ...and they bowed down and worshiped him.
> *Matthew 2:11*

Oh, that we would follow their example! "Falling to their knees, they honored him" (CEB). Though he was a child, the wise men humbled themselves in his presence and gave Jesus the respect he was due.

> Then they opened their treasures and presented
> him with gifts of gold, frankincense and myrrh.
> *Matthew 2:11*

Their presents were well chosen: gold for a king, incense for a priest, and myrrh for a burial, pointing to the sacrifice to come. God was also providing for his Son's needs and for Mary's and Joseph's as well.

Leaving the gifts at Jesus's feet, the Magi started for home by another route rather than return to Jerusalem. Herod and his demands held no sway over these Persians.

In years to come Mary surely relived every moment of their remarkable visit. The words that were spoken, the looks on their faces, the treasure chests they opened, the gifts they placed at her son's feet. The Magi are not mentioned again in Scripture. But Mary would never forget the day she welcomed them to Bethlehem.

Suppose we rejoin her just one week after she delivered Jesus. We find her bathing him in preparation for the ceremony that would mark him as a son of Israel.

On the eighth day, when it was time to circumcise the child,... *Luke 2:21*

Right, the *"b'rit-milah"* (cjb). Elizabeth went through this with little John. It wasn't merely about cutting away the foreskin. It was a physical, outward sign of a deeply spiritual truth: "My covenant in your flesh is to be an everlasting covenant."[8]

Why on the eighth day? Modern medicine gives us a clue. Eight days after a male child is born, his liver produces an elevated level of prothrombin, enabling his blood to clot properly.[9] Our wise and loving God has a purpose for everything.

When the holy child's blood was spilled, only then was his name given.

...he was named Jesus,... *Luke 2:21*

In the Old Testament, sons were named as soon as they were born. But in the New Testament, circumcision and a public naming went together, at least for John and then for our Savior. Acting on what the angels had told them, Mary and Joseph named their son Jesus, who was, and is, and is to come.

...the name the angel had given him before he was conceived. *Luke 2:21*

Luke reminds us that the name Jesus was chosen before his birth, which means it was chosen before Mary said yes. Not only did she have faith in God, but God had faith in her.

Just as God always knew how the life of his Son would unfold on earth, God knows how our lives will unfold as well. Nothing is a surprise to him. When we stumble, however badly, he stretches out his hands, pulls us to our feet, and draws us into his embrace.

His Son made that possible. We who are least worthy are most grateful.

"Peace to me is stepping into the unknown and unexpected, knowing that my Father planned every part of my life before I was born."

—RHETTA

In Bethlehem of old, Mary held the Savior of the world, gazing at her child in awe and wonder. A week before, he was growing inside her; now he was nestled in her arms.

> When the time came for the purification rites
> required by the Law of Moses,... *Luke 2:22*

A full month had passed since his circumcision. Next, Mary had to undergo a "ritual cleansing" (CEB), obeying "what the Law of Moses says a mother is supposed to do" (CEV). Namely, after the birth of a son, she had to wait forty days to be purified from her bleeding,[10] during which time she couldn't worship in a sanctuary or handle anything sacred—except God's Son.

With those forty days behind them, Mary and Joseph were free to enter the temple courts. Since Bethlehem is only five or six miles from Jerusalem, this little family probably began walking early in the morning to avoid the heat of the day. I'm imagining that Mary bore her child in a cloth slung around her shoulders, the same way I once carried our son in a Snugli, close to my heart. Warm, cozy, safe.

> …Joseph and Mary took him to Jerusalem to present
> him to the Lord… *Luke 2:22*

There's something wonderful about Jesus the Son being presented to God the Father. Though God is spirit, not flesh, at some level it must have been like looking into a mirror.

> …(as it is written in the Law of the Lord, "Every
> firstborn male is to be consecrated to the Lord"),…
> *Luke 2:23*

Because Mary and Joseph were God-fearing people, "they did exactly what was written in the Lord's Teachings" (GOD'S

WORD) and headed for the temple, where Jesus would be "set apart *and* dedicated *and* called holy to the Lord" (AMP). Though he was already holy, Jesus was treated like any other firstborn son in Israel. Though his mother was highly favored, she had to follow the necessary rituals for cleanliness.

> ...and to offer a sacrifice in keeping with what is said in the Law of the Lord: "a pair of doves or two young pigeons." *Luke 2:24*

Yet another law for a new mother to follow in order to be ceremonially clean from her flow of blood. The preferred sacrifices were a year-old lamb for a burnt offering and a young pigeon or a dove for a sin offering. But if a woman couldn't afford a lamb to sacrifice—and it's clear that Mary could not—doves or pigeons had to suffice.[11]

Think of it! Mary brought no sacrificial lamb, yet in her arms she bore the Lamb of God, who would take away the sins of the world. It's been rightly said, "No station is dishonorable where God places us."[12] Mary was humble, but she was not ashamed. She brought what she could. God asks no more than that.

The Nicanor Gate to the Court of Israel, where sacrifices were made, had been open since dawn. Joseph would have delivered Mary's two birds—domesticated, not wild, and without blemish—to be sacrificed on the altar while she waited with their infant son in the Court of Women.[13]

Did anyone take notice of her or have reason to? A poor young woman with a babe in swaddling clothes, Mary was a small-town girl, unaccustomed to the crowded temple courts. If people looked at her at all, they probably looked down on her. Yet God saw her, just as he sees us even when we feel neglected, dismissed, overlooked. "For the eyes of the LORD range throughout the earth to strengthen those whose hearts are fully committed to him."[14] That would certainly describe our Mary.

When the sacrificial service had ended and Joseph was reunited with his wife, they might have looked toward the outer gates with relief, eager to return home to Galilee and begin their lives anew. Maybe the cloud of suspicion that had hung over the early months of their marriage would evaporate when the people of Nazareth met their sweet baby boy.

Meanwhile, two people in the temple courts had been waiting a very long time to see this holy child. One of them was Anna, whom we'll meet in the next chapter. And the other was this fellow.

Now there was a man in Jerusalem called Simeon,…
Luke 2:25

He might have been named for the second son of Jacob and Leah, or his name might have been chosen because the Hebrew word *shama* means "he has heard." We're told nothing about Simeon's background other than his name. Not his tribe or his position or his family status. But we do know his spiritual condition.

> …who was righteous and devout. *Luke 2:25*

Like Zechariah, Simeon was a "just and virtuous" (WYC) man, "cautiously and carefully observing the divine Law" (AMP). Yet unlike Zechariah, who required proof of God's goodness, Simeon was simply listening and waiting. His ear was tuned to the Lord's voice. Daily his eyes scanned the horizon for the Messiah he knew was coming.

> He was waiting for the consolation of Israel,…
> *Luke 2:25*

Usually we console people who are sorrowful or have lost someone dear to them. What had the people of God lost? They'd lost their way, just as we have in our generation. We turn to one another for answers, when God alone can provide the wisdom we need. We depend upon possessions or position to sustain us, when both can be swept away like chaff on the wind, leaving us empty handed.

As for the Israelites, they'd pursued false gods, worshiped idols, turned their backs on the Almighty, and done what was right in their own eyes. Now they needed to be consoled and longed to be redeemed. Just as we do.

Save us, Lord. Save us from ourselves.

For centuries God's people had been "eagerly waiting for the Messiah to come and rescue Israel" (NLT). In Hebrew, *Messiah* means "Anointed One," as does the Greek word *Christos*. Through the Lord Jesus would come "the restoration of Israel" (CEB).

That's why our good Simeon was waiting for the Messiah. But lots of people passed through the temple courts in Jerusalem. How did Simeon recognize the Christ child?

…and the Holy Spirit was on him. *Luke 2:25*

Ah. It wasn't Simeon's goodness or even his patience that enabled him to see the Lord's Anointed. "His heart was open to the Holy Spirit" (PHILLIPS). The same Holy Spirit that came upon Mary. The same Holy Spirit that filled Elizabeth, Zechariah, and their son, John. The same Holy Spirit at work in the lives of believers today. "God's love has been poured out into our hearts through the Holy Spirit, who has been given to us."[15]

The Holy Spirit opens eyes and ears. Where there is darkness, he sheds light. He reveals truth. And he speaks about the future with authority.

Simeon's very life was dependent on the Spirit.

> It had been revealed to him by the Holy Spirit that he would not die before he had seen the Lord's Messiah.
>
> *Luke 2:26*

The Holy Spirit "divinely told him" (YLT). Okay, but *how?* Audible voice? Writing on the wall? Star in the heavens? Angelic visit? Burning bush? Talking donkey? Vivid dream? Since the days of Adam and Eve, God has used all those creative methods of communication. When the Holy Spirit reveals, there is no mistaking the Source and no second-guessing the message. It rings like a bell in our hearts: a single, clear note. *Yes.*

Simeon knew the revelation was from the Lord, who assured Simeon "he would not die before he had seen God's Chosen One" (NLV). Simeon had anticipated this moment, knowing full well that death might swiftly follow his holy sighting. A real Catch-22—unless the man had no fear of dying.

Maybe because of that reference to death, both scholars and laypeople have assumed Simeon was old, though his age is not mentioned in the Bible. He could have been thirty or fifty or seventy. Or, yes, ninety.

"Many times I've thought someone younger should be doing the ministries I do, but I can see that God's timing is perfect, and this is my time to serve in whatever capacity I can."

—KAREN

What we know absolutely is that Simeon was led by the Holy Spirit and so was given the ability "to speak things above himself,"[16] things he could not have known without divine revelation.

> Moved by the Spirit, he went into the temple courts.
> *Luke 2:27*

Since Mary was on hand, this would have been "that part of the temple where the public worship was chiefly performed— into the court of the women."[17] We can almost feel Simeon's heart racing as he hurried across the broad, open courtyard, "guided by the Spirit" (NRSV). *Show me, Lord. Point the way. I know the Messiah is here!*

> When the parents brought in the child Jesus to
> do for him what the custom of the Law required,...
> *Luke 2:27*

My, the Law has been emphasized a great deal in a few verses. God wants us to know that his Son honored the Law of Moses since he came not only to fulfill it but to surpass it: "For the law was given through Moses; grace and truth came through Jesus Christ."[18]

Mary and Joseph were surely caught off guard, having come to Jerusalem simply to do what the Law "says should be done for a new baby" (CEV).

All at once this smiling stranger greeted them and claimed their son.

...Simeon took him in his arms... *Luke 2:28*

Stop right there. If a complete stranger walked up and tried to lift my newborn child out of my embrace, I would turn into a growling mama bear in a heartbeat. Only the Holy Spirit could have opened Mary's arms to allow Simeon to take him.

Maybe it was the man's eyes, alight with God's love. Or his smile, bright as the sun. Perhaps there were tears glistening on Simeon's cheeks or a gentleness in his manner that engendered Mary's trust. No doubt some were standing about, nodding their approval, knowing this man's reputation far better than Mary could and so giving her confidence.

However he managed it, Simeon "received him into his arms" (ASV) and drew the child "as near his heart as he could, which was as full of joy as it could hold."[19] Whether he'd waited in anticipation the whole of his life or only since the Messiah was conceived, Simeon could not wait another moment to give thanks.

> …and praised God, saying:… *Luke 2:28*

Simeon got the memo: open mouth, praise God.

> …"Sovereign Lord, as you have promised,…"
> *Luke 2:29*

In more than half the English translations, Simeon's words appear in poetic verse rather than a paragraph of text. Another song, then. Another exuberant expression prompted by the Holy Spirit. And another Latin name, *Nunc Dimittis,* for the opening words of his canticle, "Now you dismiss."

Simeon wisely began by acknowledging God's sovereignty, calling him "Master" (NRSV), "Ruler" (KNOX), and "King over all" (NIrV). Then he reminded the Lord that, "according to your word" (CEB), he was more than willing to die a happy man.

"…you may now dismiss your servant in peace."
Luke 2:29

Woody Allen once said, "I'm not afraid of death. I just don't want to be there when it happens." Simeon was there. He'd prepared for this moment and was definitely ready to "leave this world" (AMP).

"Realizing that God's timing is perfect helps me to trust more and more in him and not question why things happen the way they do."

— SHERRY

How could Simeon be so calm in the face of death? Because he knew Israel was safely in God's hands. And so was he.

"For my eyes have seen your salvation,…" *Luke 2:30*

Simeon was looking at a baby no more than six weeks old. He was also looking at eternity. By the power of the Holy Spirit, Simeon saw it all. The cross. The grave. The resurrection. "My eyes have seen the One Who will save men from the punishment of their sins" (NLV), he proclaimed. Yet another confession of faith—like Elizabeth's, like Mary's—spoken three decades before the start of Christ's earthly ministry. "My own eyes have seen that saving power of thine" (KNOX), Simeon told the Lord he loved.

Do you see what I see? Miracles upon miracles. There are so many angelic appearances, so many prophecies fulfilled, so many lives changed by the Spirit of the Lord that if we didn't know God's Word to be trustworthy, we might think the whole story was too fantastic to be believed. Ah, but "What the LORD says is right and true. He is faithful in everything he does."[20] This is no fairy tale, no legend, no bedtime story. This is the real Christmas. The Messiah come to set his people free.

> "…which you have prepared in the sight of all
> nations:…" *Luke 2:31*

From Simeon's viewpoint "it's now out in the open for everyone to see" (MSG). Even so, some people were strolling past them in the temple courts, too self-absorbed to notice good and godly Simeon, let alone recognize the Savior in his arms.

Only when we're filled with the Holy Spirit can we see what matters to God.

> "…a light for revelation to the Gentiles…"
> *Luke 2:32*

Talk about looking into eternity! Simeon let this stunned mother and father know that their child had come for "the Gentiles as well as Israel."[21] The prophet Isaiah had spoken the same truth centuries earlier, writing of One who would be "a light for the Gentiles."[22]

"…and the glory of your people Israel." *Luke 2:32*

More light, more "shining-greatness" (NLV) bringing "praise *and* honor *and* glory to Your people Israel" (AMP). This was definitely the Holy Spirit talking. The message was profound, the words eloquent. Like the other three prophetic songs we've heard from Elizabeth, Mary, and Zechariah—the first Christmas carols, if you will—Simeon's lyrical outburst must have drawn quite a crowd.

The child's father and mother marveled at what was said about him. *Luke 2:33*

Whether or not they recalled Isaiah's prophecy when they heard it, Mary and Joseph were "amazed" (CEB) and left "wondering over all that was said of him" (KNOX). Really, who could take it all in? Ten months earlier Mary had heard a mind-boggling report from an angel about a son she would bear.

Soon after, so did Joseph. But this was a respected man in the temple courts calling their baby the light of the world.

If we were filming this, the camera would slowly pull back, still focused on their "astonished" (LEB) expressions, letting us see this humble couple, dressed in the simple clothes of the countryside, standing among a crowd that included the sophisticated people of Jerusalem in their finest attire.

A poor couple among the rich? No. A rich couple among the poor. In Simeon's arms lay the finest treasure the world will ever know.

> Then Simeon blessed them and said to Mary, his mother:... *Luke 2:34*

First, he "said a bracha over them" (OJB), a blessing meant for both parents. But the words that followed were specifically for Mary. Perhaps, by the Spirit's leading, Simeon knew that Joseph was not the child's biological father. Or Simeon might have wanted to prepare this young mother for the heartache to come.

> ..."This child is destined to cause the falling and rising of many in Israel,..." *Luke 2:34*

Why was this ominous-sounding prophecy directed at Mary? Because God wished it so. He knew her heart, knew what she could bear. Also, Joseph is not mentioned at the end of Christ's earthly ministry. Perhaps he did not live long enough to see that "many people in Israel will be condemned and many others will be saved" (GOD'S WORD) because of their child.

Strong words, and Simeon wasn't finished yet.

> "…and to be a sign that will be spoken against,…"
> *Luke 2:34*

Oh dear. Jesus would bear much influence, but he would not always be liked. In fact, he would be "like a warning sign" (CEV), certain to be "misunderstood and contradicted" (MSG), the kind of man "that generates opposition" (CEB). Before all was said and done, Simeon cautioned Mary that "many people will reject him" (CEV).

Difficult words for any mother to hear. This stranger, however kind, had gone from praising God to prophesying a gloomy future for her son.

> "…so that the thoughts of many hearts will be revealed." *Luke 2:35*

He too would be a prophet then, probing people's "inner thoughts" (CEB), showing "what people are really thinking" (CEV). Yes, that sounds like the Lord, all right. When we come face to face with Jesus, there's no point trying to hide our true feelings. "What people think will be made known" (WE). Because the Lord loves those who are his, he breaks us open, reveals our darkness, and offers the cleansing power of his grace.

But for those who don't want their sins exposed, such a prophet would be unwelcome. True then, true now.

> "And a sword will pierce your own soul too."
> *Luke 2:35*

Did Simeon lower his voice when he said this? Or gently place the Christ child in Mary's arms, offering immediate solace? Surely he did something to lighten the heavy blow when he said, "And you, Mary, will suffer as though you had been stabbed by a dagger" (CEV). Indeed, dear Mary, "sorrow, like a sharp sword, will break your own heart" (GNT).

The same word is used in 1 Samuel 17:51 to describe the large broadsword carried by Goliath, the giant.[23] Not a theoretical sword or a ceremonial one hanging on a wall in Herod's palace. A real sword. A deadly weapon.

"Fear of tomorrow crouches at the door, but I know that God is in charge and has a plan."

—CATHY

I'm grateful Mary didn't know that day what her son's future held. At the end of his short life, Jesus would be crucified, the most ignoble and humiliating of deaths. While he hung on the cross, a sharp blade would be thrust into his side, "bringing a sudden flow of blood and water."[24] Mary would watch every agonizing moment. She would surely feel the point of that blade as if it were piercing her own flesh.

Oh, Mary, dear Mary. You've already sacrificed your body to bear God's child.

She never could have imagined that the hardest sacrifice was yet to come. That day in Jerusalem, Mary must have reeled from the impact of Simeon's remarks. Wonderful news at first, followed by terrible news. *A sword. A sword.*

Those were Simeon's last recorded words. Though the Scriptures don't tell us, he might have died within the hour—at peace, his mission fulfilled, his work completed. Or he might have lived another decade, praising God.

"When the circumstances of life threaten to overwhelm me, I remember Mary's response to God's appointed plan—one that meant great cost to her, one of suffering and not understanding all God was doing. Her example of simple but complete trust has encouraged me through some difficult hours."

—ROBIN

If your heart has grown heavy, thinking of all young Mary had to bear, be at peace. Her story is not quite done.

At that very moment in the temple courts, a woman stepped forward when she was needed most. To comfort Mary and assure her that God had not forgotten her—would never forget her—just as he will never forget any one of us.

For all those Mary moments, when fear clouds our thinking and the future looks grim, consider the words of Peter, who knew and loved Mary's son, Jesus: "Cast all your anxiety on him because he cares for you."[25] He does, beloved. Truly, he does.

Eight

Come, thou long expected Jesus,
Born to set thy people free;
From our fears and sins release us,
Let us find our rest in thee.
Israel's strength and consolation,
Hope of all the earth thou art;
Dear desire of every nation,
Joy of every longing heart.

—Charles Wesley, "Come, Thou
Long Expected Jesus," 1745

Joy of Every
Longing Heart

ary was standing in the temple court with the Christ child in her embrace when he was "taken notice of by one Anna."[1] A singular individual. A one-of-a-kind woman, unique in the Bible.

I'm rather in awe of Anna. No, it's more than that. She intimidates me. And compels me to press on, "grasping ever more firmly that purpose for which Christ grasped me."[2]

We've all met women who make us think, *I want to be like her when I grow up.* She's plugged into life, whatever her age. She keeps informed; she stays involved; she reaches beyond her comfort zone; she cares deeply about people. Above all, she has a vibrant relationship with God that shines around her like sunlight.

That's Anna, our final woman of Christmas.

There was also a prophet, Anna,... *Luke 2:36*

Yes, a *female* prophet—in Hebrew, *neviah* or "prophetess" (OJB)—a rare creature in Scripture. You'll find only a handful of them mentioned: Miriam, Deborah, Huldah, Noadiah, the wife of Isaiah, and in the New Testament the daughters of Philip the evangelist.[3]

And now Anna, "a woman who spoke God's Word" (NLV). Like the name Hannah in Hebrew, the Greek name Anna means "favor" or "grace." Lovely.

> …the daughter of Penuel, of the tribe of Asher.
> *Luke 2:36*

The family name speaks well for her upbringing. Penuel means "face of God." As for her tribe, Asher settled in western Galilee during the time of Joshua.[4] Some tribe members clearly made their way to Jerusalem, because that's where we find Anna.

> She was very old;… *Luke 2:36*

Very old. Like Sarah. Like Elizabeth. We know better than to discount Anna just because she was "far advanced in years" (DRA). These women and others are part of a long tradition in which God "particularly favors older women as channels of divine grace."[5] Anna didn't give birth beyond her childbearing season, but wait until you see the fertile seeds she planted for the kingdom.

"What a mighty God we have, to value us no matter our age, status, or outward appearance!"

— CHRISTINA

Compared to the limited information given about Simeon, we have an abundance of detail about Anna.

> …she had lived with her husband seven years after her marriage,… *Luke 2:36*

Alas, then he died. Our hearts sink at the thought of a young woman—in her early twenties at most—losing her husband "seven years from her maidenhood" (AMP). From that sad day forward, she soldiered on as an unmarried widow. If she had living family members, they are not mentioned in Scripture.

> …and then was a widow until she was eighty-four. *Luke 2:37*

All these numbers intrigue me. And they jive with something I've noticed of late. When I chat with women in their forties and fifties, they seldom mention their exact age. But once a woman crosses an invisible line, around age sixty, she is quick to say, "Now that I'm sixty-three..." or "When you get to be seventy-five..." A woman's age becomes a badge of courage. *I have made it this far, and I am not done yet!*

Many illustrious women appeared on the world stage during Anna's long lifetime: Cleopatra, the last pharaoh of ancient Egypt; Mariamne, the beautiful and tragic second wife of Herod; Olivia, the Empress Consort of Rome.[6] Anna's name may not be found among theirs in the history books, but it's surely written in the book of life.[7] Her story endures because of who she worshiped and how faithfully she did so.

Some translations tell us "she was a widow for eighty-four years" (NCV), which would make her more than a century old. Others say she was "fourscore and four years" (KJV), or eighty-four—the precise age of my dear mother-in-law as I write these words. I certainly don't think of Mary Lee Higgs as very old. Even with eighty-four candles on her birthday cake, she is full of life and full of fun.

"In every season of life, we have worth as servants of the Lord."

— CATHY

Anna's senior citizenship isn't shown here as a negative. Whatever her age, "Anna was young in hope."[8] Her marital

status, though, was a definite challenge. In those days a child-
less widow had little choice but to return to her parents' home,
where she waited to marry again or to die, whichever came
first.[9] With no means of earning money, such women depended on the support of family and friends,[10] often living in
poverty.

But Anna was an independent-minded widow, the sort
"who lives in the Temple and devotes herself to her spiritual
life."[11] She was that ideal widow Paul later talked about: "The
widow who is really in need and left all alone puts her hope in
God and continues night and day to pray and to ask God for
help."[12] That's our Anna. She ran to God and gave him her
broken heart, pledging her life to his service.

She never left the temple but... *Luke 2:37*

Wait. *Never?* Never. "Anna was always at the Temple"
(ERV). Though Herod's Temple in Jerusalem was enormous—
roughly sixteen hundred feet by a thousand feet[13]—it still
would be rather confining to spend every waking and sleeping
hour in one place. Yet Anna could not bring herself to "go away
from the house of God" (NLV).

Picture four enclosed courtyards in succession, "each more
exclusive than the one before it."[14] First came the Court of the
Gentiles, which anyone was permitted to enter. Then the Court

of Women, the Court of Israel, and finally the Court of the Priests.

Naturally, Anna was relegated to the Court of Women and probably lived in one of the four rooms built in the corners.[15] A single room, no doubt plainly furnished for this devout woman who was "more interested in unseen things of the spirit than in material, tangible possessions."[16]

For Anna, the temple in Jerusalem was her home. It was where she belonged. She "typified the Jerusalem Temple woman at her noblest,"[17] investing her time and resources in serving the Almighty. We can almost hear her whispering the words of David, perhaps even singing them:

> One thing I ask from the LORD,
>   this only do I seek:
> that I may dwell in the house of the LORD
>   all the days of my life,
> to gaze on the beauty of the LORD
>   and to seek him in his temple.[18]

And what did Anna do in that temple? How did she spend all the minutes, hours, days, months, and years of her long life? She did what gave her the greatest joy.

> …worshiped night and day,… *Luke 2:37*

Interesting that the words *served* and *worshiped* are used interchangeably here, depending on the translation. "She worshiped God" (ERV); "she served God" (CEV). Well, we do call it a *worship service.*

Anna worshiped night and day. All the time. "Continually—that is, at the usual times of public worship and in private."[19] Surely the woman slept—all mortals must—but even then she might have dreamed of being in God's presence.

When she was awake, Anna engaged in two disciplines embraced by people of God the world over.

...fasting and praying. *Luke 2:37*

This was her worship. This was her service. Sometimes the word *fasting* here is shown as plural—"fastings" (KJV)—letting us see the start-and-stop nature of her fasts. She wasn't starving herself; she was simply "going without food so she could pray better" (NLV). Anna was serious about honoring the Lord, about seeking his face, about praising his name. She fasted. And she prayed. Offering "supplications" (ASV) on behalf of others, "Anna became an intercessor for the ages."[20]

"I've fasted and prayed and worshiped, yes, but this woman made it her life!"

—CHRISTINA

Such activities, then and now, are often done in seclusion, even in silence, and without applause. Could I do that? Serve in solitude without anyone praising my efforts? Alas, I know the answer.

Years ago as an unmarried woman, I cleaned an apartment building to help pay my rent. It was a Victorian house with long wooden staircases between floors. I still recall sitting on the top landing, dust rag in hand, sighing heavily as I looked down all those steps. When I was about halfway through the painstaking process of running my rag over each intricately carved post, removing what appeared to be months of dust, a tenant passed me on the stair without a single word of thanks.

What did I expect? I was working for his landlord, not for him. Still, I felt unseen and unimportant.

And so I look at Anna and am utterly humbled by her willingness to gaze in only one direction: upward. As Paul later wrote in his first letter to the church at Corinth, "An unmarried woman or virgin is concerned about the Lord's affairs: Her aim is to be devoted to the Lord in both body and spirit."[21] Body and spirit. Fasting and praying. Anna was "always in a praying frame"[22] and had a "strangely expectant faith."[23]

As far as we know, Simeon and Anna were not related except in their shared longing to see the Messiah. "They knew every prophecy from Isaiah to Malachi and looked every day for the Lord's Christ."[24] Why did God have both these people waiting at the temple? To show us that Jesus came for everyone, men and women, so that "one of each sex might bear witness to him."[25]

Simeon's life was complete now that he'd laid eyes on the Savior. But Anna's ministry had just kicked into high gear. She was standing nearby when she saw Simeon holding a babe and praising God. Her heart must have leaped for joy. *The Messiah!* "God, who had cared for her so faithfully all these years, saw to it that she didn't miss that sacred moment."[26]

All at once Anna was on the move.

> Coming up to them at that very moment,...
> *Luke 2:38*

Some of us are hesitant in nature, more likely to observe than to act. Anna was not that woman. She stepped up and spoke up "in that instant" (NKJV). Indeed, "at the very time Simeon was praying" (MSG) or perhaps a moment later when "Simeon was talking to Mary, Anna also came along" (WE).

She knew. *She knew.* In the same way and for the same reason that Elizabeth knew: the Holy Spirit revealed to our prophetess that this was indeed the Christ.

...she gave thanks to God... Luke 2:38

Anna got the memo too: open mouth, praise God.

If we did this one thing—*this one thing*—it would change our lives and the lives of those around us forever. If we blessed God openly and regularly, if we gave him credit instead of taking it for ourselves, if the first thing that came to mind and mouth was glorifying his name, we too might catch a glimpse of the Christ, as Anna did when she "broke into an anthem of praise to God" (MSG).

Anna not only lifted her voice to the Lord; she also proclaimed the truth of the Messiah with joyous abandon.

...and spoke about the child to all... Luke 2:38

Oh yes, she "talked about Jesus" (ERV) to everyone who would listen and especially "to all who have longed for his appearing."[27]

...who were looking forward to the redemption of Jerusalem. Luke 2:38

Seasoned as she was, Anna knew all the temple regulars—the priests and the worshipers, the Pharisees and the faithful.

She knew who had ears to hear and eyes to see, and so she made sure to tell those people about Jesus. *All* of them, the Word says. "All who were waiting expectantly" (MOUNCE), all who were "looking for the One to save them from the punishment of their sins" (NLV).

Three decades ago I was looking for the One who could forgive me, the One who could restore me. When I discovered his name was Jesus, when I realized he was born so that we might be born again…well, I haven't stopped talking about him since! Anna too couldn't keep the good news to herself. "When no-one else in authority was proclaiming the birth of the Messiah, this old woman was telling the world."[28]

Yes, she was old, but she was also bold. Just as she'd stepped up to greet Mary and Joseph, she quickly moved forward to address everyone else. Did she approach people one by one or stand before crowds? The Greek simply says she *spoke.* Yet I keep circling back to the word *all* and the fact that she was a prophetess, unafraid of speaking up and speaking out. However she managed it, in public venues or in private discussions, many people in Jerusalem heard about the Messiah's birth, proclaimed by a woman who'd attained "the status of wise and holy elder."[29]

I think it's safe to say Anna was further down the path than most of us and not just in years. These few verses reveal a woman of exceptional devotion, incredible discipline, and endless dedication. Her example continues to inspire God's daughters from generation to generation. Just as Elizabeth's story does. And Mary's.

As David once wrote, "The Lord announces the word, and the women who proclaim it are a mighty throng."[30] Amen to that! Elizabeth, Mary, and Anna are among that mighty throng who've heard God's truth and gladly given him the glory.

"I want to be willing to be used by God just like each of these women of Christmas: to know the Holy Spirit is with me like Elizabeth, to ponder in my heart like Mary, and to be completely devoted to the Lord's service like Anna."

—TINA

In the end the women of Christmas quietly stepped aside, making room for the One who truly matters. The Hero of our story.

> And the child grew and became strong;…
> *Luke 2:40*

Not strong like Samson. Jesus "waxed strong in Spirit" (GNV). His carpentry work developed his muscular strength, but he needed far more than that to do his Father's work. He soon became "a mature young man" (ERV), spiritually strong beyond his years.

...he was filled with wisdom,... *Luke 2:40*

Rather than being born with that wisdom, the Christ child was filled with it by his heavenly Father, like water poured into a jar. As he grew physically, his mind stretched to learn new truths. Jesus was not born speaking, feeding himself, or walking. He had to grow, inside and out. He had to be made like us, "fully human in every way,"[31] yet without sin so that one day he could fully atone for our sins.

Mary's humble offering of two doves couldn't begin to cover the sins I've committed just in the last twenty-four hours, let alone the whole of my life. Only the blood of Jesus can do that. Only the grace of his heavenly Father.

...and the grace of God was on him. *Luke 2:40*

On him and in him and through him. Grace and mercy and favor. "God loved him, and cherished him, and took a particular care of him."[32] By the power of the Holy Spirit, the women of Christmas did their part, anticipating the Lord's advent, dedicating their lives to his service, and honoring his sacred name even before he was born.

Now it falls to us, two thousand years later, to follow in their footsteps.

To tell everyone we know everything we know about Jesus. To say words such as *miracle* and *angel* without apology, because they're true. To see the light of Christ shining through the ages and lift our candles to light the way for others.

To join the heavenly host singing "Glory, glory, glory! Glory to God in the highest!"

Amen and amen.

Study Guide

If you're ready to examine the stories of Elizabeth, Mary, and Anna more closely—on your own or in a small-group setting—this study guide is designed for just that purpose.

You'll need a place to write your answers—a notebook, a computer, whatever works best for you—and the willingness to explore both Scripture and your own heart at a deeper level.

You might begin reading *The Women of Christmas* in early November and study one chapter a week throughout the festive season. Or read two chapters each Sunday of Advent. Or you could immerse yourself in one chapter a day during the week leading up to Christmas. Whatever your preference, I pray your holiday will take on a fuller, richer meaning because of the time you've spent with these exceptional women. And I hope the lessons you've learned will stay with you long after you've rung in the New Year.

Chapter One: Let Every Heart Prepare Him Room

Read Luke 1:5–18.

1. Elizabeth is described as righteous, blameless, and honorable. Look through Proverbs 31:10–31, then

choose the verses that best describe how a godly woman in biblical times might have lived out her faith in practical, day-to-day ways. If you know a modern Elizabeth, what specific things does she do that you find exemplary? How might these women from the past and present inspire you to change the way you'll serve God in the future?

2. Elizabeth's goodness came from God and glorified God, as we find in 2 Peter 1:3: "His divine power has given us everything we need for a godly life through our knowledge of him who called us by his own glory and goodness." What happens when we praise ourselves—if only in our minds—when we do something right? How can you combat the very human urge to take credit for your good behavior, when it belongs solely to God?

3. When Zechariah was bewildered and alarmed by the appearance of a heavenly messenger, the angel told him, "Do not be afraid." When and where in your life might you need a reminder that God does everything out of love so you truly can put aside your fears? What comfort might you find in Isaiah 12:2: "Surely God is my salvation; I will trust and not be afraid. The LORD,

the LORD himself, is my strength and my defense; he has become my salvation"? And how might John 14:27 encourage you: "Peace I leave with you; my peace I give you. I do not give to you as the world gives. Do not let your hearts be troubled and do not be afraid"?

Chapter Two: Let All Mortal Flesh Keep Silence

Read Luke 1:19–25.

1. R. C. Sproul said of the angel Gabriel, "Such a one should be believed."[1] Yet because Zechariah didn't believe, Elizabeth spent all nine months of her pregnancy with a husband who could not speak or hear. In what ways might that lengthy silence have been a challenge for these two—individually and as a married couple? And how might it have been an unexpected blessing? If the Lord silenced you even for a day, what lessons might you learn?

2. On pages 31–32 you'll find several possible reasons why Elizabeth remained in seclusion for five months. Which one of the many suggestions seems most plausible to you, and why? Now read Psalm 139:13–16, which describes God's participation in forming an unborn child, beginning with "For you created my inmost being; you

knit me together in my mother's womb." How might those verses add deeper meaning to Elizabeth's statement, "The Lord has done this for me"?

3. In Ecclesiastes 7:8 we learn, "The end of a matter is better than its beginning, and patience is better than pride." In what ways does Elizabeth's story illustrate that truth? If you too are waiting for a particular blessing from God, how does Elizabeth's story challenge you? encourage you? convict you? give you hope?

Chapter Three: The Virgin Mother Kind

Read Luke 1:26–38.

1. Because of Mary's unique role in God's story, it's easy to put her on a pedestal and walk away, convinced she has nothing to teach mere mortals like us. Yet we see how very human she was in her scene with Gabriel when she asked, "How will this be, since I am a virgin?" What questions might you have had for Gabriel if you'd stood in Mary's sandals that day? Perhaps Mary's youthful innocence contributed to her simple yet solid faith. How can we lay aside our cynicism and recapture our ability to take the Lord at his Word and trust him completely?

2. The prophet Jeremiah confessed, "Ah, Sovereign LORD, you have made the heavens and the earth by your great power and outstretched arm. Nothing is too hard for you."[2] What things in your life *seem* too hard to handle? Make a list. Then write across the top your favorite translation of Luke 1:37. If you truly believe that nothing is impossible with God, what must you do right now to embrace that reality?

3. One author said of Mary's willingness to bear God's son, "Right from the start, the cost was high. So were the risks."[3] What did Mary's obedience cost her from the moment she said yes? And what risks was she taking for the future? What would it take for you to say with all your heart, "I live to do God's will"?[4] Consider how 1 John 2:17 might strengthen your resolve: "The world and its desires pass away, but whoever does the will of God lives forever."

Chapter Four: O Tidings of Comfort and Joy

Read Luke 1:39–56.

1. Soon after Gabriel's departure, Mary headed for Elizabeth's house, the angel's words surely echoing in her heart: *You who are highly favored.* Think of a

time when you felt favored or blessed by God. Were
you eager to share that experience with others? Why
or why not? Did Mary need to *give* something to—
or *get* something from—Elizabeth? How might
each of them have benefited from their three-month
visit?

2. Though Elizabeth was a good deal older than Mary,
they were hugely supportive of each other. If you have
a younger—or older—woman in your life who builds
up your faith, how does she accomplish that? And
how do you build up hers? What steps might you
take to strengthen and enhance your spiritual relationship with others of a different generation?

3. In the end neither Elizabeth nor Mary is the star of
this chapter; rather, the Holy Spirit takes center stage.
In John 14:26 we learn that the Holy Spirit "will
teach you all things." In Acts 13:4 Barnabas and Saul
were "sent on their way by the Holy Spirit." And in
Romans 15:13 we're told we will "overflow with hope
by the power of the Holy Spirit." What role does the
Holy Spirit play in your life? When and where have
you sensed God's Spirit teaching you? sending you?
flowing through you?

Chapter Five: With Heart and Soul and Voice

Read Luke 1:57–79 and Matthew 1:18–25.

1. If Zechariah's silence wasn't punishment, it still might have been God's discipline, as we read in Job 5:17, "Blessed is the one whom God corrects," and in Proverbs 3:12, "The LORD disciplines those he loves." How would you describe the difference between punishment and correction? When have you been aware that God was disciplining you, and what did you learn from the experience?

2. When he could speak again, Zechariah's first impulse was to praise God. It's easy to honor God when we're happy, grateful, and content, yet God is equally worthy of our praise when we're disappointed, sorrowful, or angry, just as Psalm 42:5 teaches us: "Why, my soul, are you downcast? Why so disturbed within me? Put your hope in God, for I will yet praise him, my Savior and my God." Do you think praising God is more for our benefit or for his? How does the act of praising him change your attitude or perspective?

3. One commentator wrote, "Joseph's obedience and submission...is scarcely less remarkable than Mary's."[5]

How was Joseph's original plan to quietly divorce Mary still a display of mercy? When instead he married her, as the angel commanded, did Joseph become a true hero in your eyes? If so, what qualities make him admirable, even remarkable? Though Joseph never speaks in the Bible, the Word tells us, "the LORD is a God who knows, and by him deeds are weighed."[6] In your own life are you more likely to *talk* about God or to be *obedient* to God's commands? Think of a time when God asked you to step out in faithful obedience. How did you respond? And what was the outcome?

Chapter Six: The Wondrous Gift Is Given

Read Luke 2:1–20.

1. Jesus's death on the cross spans many chapters in the New Testament, yet his birth is captured in a half-dozen words with no real description of the time, the setting, the number of people on hand, or any details other than the location, Bethlehem. Why might that be so? Now imagine you are sitting across from someone who has no knowledge of Jesus. How would you tell this person the story of Christmas?

Which element of the Lord's birth impacts you most, and why?

2. God could have come to earth in any form he wished. Why do you think he chose to come as a weak and vulnerable infant, entirely dependent on others? In Mark 10:14, Jesus tells his disciples, "Let the little children come to me, and do not hinder them, for the kingdom of God belongs to such as these." What are some of the admirable qualities that children have? In what ways could you become more childlike in your faith?

3. Ever since that first Christmas night, when thousands of angels sang praises to God, music has been an integral part of the season. Choose a favorite carol, and write out the first verse. (If you're brave—or by yourself!—you might sing it aloud.) Do the lyrics accurately portray what you've read in Scripture? How do centuries of customs and traditions from around the world enhance our appreciation of this holy season? And how do they distract us from the true story of the Messiah come to earth? What plans are you making to put Christ at the center of your Christmas this year?

Chapter Seven: And Our Eyes at Last Shall See Him

Read Matthew 2:1–12 and Luke 2:21–35.

1. We know nothing of Simeon except the meaning of his name, "he has heard," and the attitude of his heart, "devout." What would you need to know about someone before you invited him or her to attend your weekly Bible study? join your family for Christmas dinner? take your newborn son from your embrace? In John 13:35, Jesus told his followers, "By this everyone will know that you are my disciples, if you love one another." How might Simeon have shown Joseph and Mary the love of God? And how might you show God's love to a stranger who crosses your path?

2. Once again the Holy Spirit played a quiet but significant part in the story, revealing to Simeon that he wouldn't die until he saw the Messiah. Would such knowledge fill you with hopeful anticipation or fearfulness and dread? How could Simeon so blithely say to God, "You may now dismiss your servant"? What would make that easy for you to say? And what would make it especially difficult? How can you best prepare for the day you see your Savior face to face?

3. Simeon's cryptic message for Mary must have taken her aback. *A sword will pierce my soul?* Since Mary was one to ponder things, how do you suppose she handled those words at the time and in the years that followed? Since we know God does all things for our good, how might Simeon's painful yet prophetic word have helped Mary? When people bring you troubling news or offer a word of caution, how do you respond to them, and what might you ask of God?

Chapter Eight: Joy of Every Longing Heart

Read Luke 2:36–40.

1. Just as Anna "turned her loneliness into 'aloneness' with God,"[7] we all have seasons when we're on our own and could use that solitude to deepen our relationship with God. Even those of us who share our lives with others have a few moments entirely to ourselves in any given day. How do you usually spend that time? What portion would you consider giving solely to God, and how might you do so?

2. Though Psalm 23:6 was written by David, his words could easily have been spoken by Anna: "Surely your

goodness and love will follow me all the days of my life, and I will dwell in the house of the LORD forever." How did Anna's faithfulness—remaining in the temple, constantly praying and fasting—strike you? Beautiful? Fanatical? How might a modern woman follow her example? Though most of us would find it difficult to mirror her 24/7 devotion, which aspect of Anna's worship challenges you to go deeper? Could you serve in some new way at your church? add more prayer time to your calendar? explore the spiritual discipline of fasting? In what ways might God be asking you to dwell more closely with him in the year ahead?

3. Elizabeth, Mary, and Anna were ordinary women blessed by God because of his goodness and used by God to accomplish extraordinary things. Think of the women you know well. Is there an Elizabeth among them? a Mary? an Anna? This holy season why not reach out to those women and tell them how they serve as role models to you? Even a personal note in a Christmas card might encourage them. Then take a moment to write a note to yourself regarding each of our Women of Christmas:

"I am most like _____

because _____."

"I learned the most from _____

because _____."

"I'd love to be more like _____

because _____."

God bless you for investing your time wisely in studying his Word. May it bear much fruit, this season and always. Merry Christmas, my sister!

Notes

Chapter 1: Let Every Heart Prepare Him Room

1. 1 Chronicles 24:10.
2. 2 Chronicles 31:2.
3. Tremper Longman III, Mark L. Strauss, and Daniel Taylor, contributors, *The Expanded Bible: Explore the Depths of the Scriptures While You Read* (Nashville: Thomas Nelson, 2011), note on Luke 1:5.
4. Edith Deen, *All of the Women of the Bible* (New York: Harper and Row, 1955), 168.
5. Ephesians 2:10.
6. R. C. Sproul, ed., *The Reformation Study Bible* (Lake Mary, FL: Ligonier, 2005), 1453, comment on Luke 1:6.
7. Psalm 127:3, CEB.
8. Catherine Clark Kroeger and Mary J. Evans, eds., "Luke," in *The IVP Women's Bible Commentary* (Downers Grove, IL: InterVarsity, 2002), 564.
9. Ross Saunders, *Outrageous Women, Outrageous God: Women in the First Two Generations of Christianity* (Alexandria, New South Wales, Australia: E. J. Dwyer, 1996), 67.
10. Carol Meyers, gen. ed., *Women in Scripture: A Dictionary of Named and Unnamed Women in the Hebrew Bible, the Apocryphal/Deuterocanonical Books, and the New Testament* (New York: Houghton Mifflin, 2000), 73.
11. Sproul, *The Reformation Study Bible,* 1453, comment on Luke 1:7.
12. Exodus 30:7–8.

13. Walter L. Liefeld, "Luke," in *The Expositor's Bible Commentary* (Grand Rapids: Zondervan, 1984), 8:826.

14. *Matthew Henry's Commentary on the Whole Bible* (Peabody, MA: Hendrickson, 1991), 5:467.

15. Psalm 141:2.

16. Luke 2:37.

17. Sproul, *The Reformation Study Bible,* 1453, comment on Luke 1:9.

18. *Matthew Henry's Commentary,* 5:466.

19. Exodus 25:30.

20. Liefeld, "Luke," 8:826.

21. Howard F. Vos, *Nelson's New Illustrated Bible Manners and Customs: How the People of the Bible Really Lived* (Nashville: Thomas Nelson, 1999), 383.

22. Margaret E. Sangster, *The Women of the Bible: A Portrait Gallery* (New York: Christian Herald, 1911), 259.

23. Psalm 127:4, RSV.

24. Sproul, *The Reformation Study Bible,* 1453, comment on Luke 1:13.

25. Matthew 3:3.

26. Frances Vander Velde, *Women of the Bible* (Grand Rapids: Kregel, 1985), 152.

27. Rose Sallberg Kam, *Their Stories, Our Stories: Women of the Bible* (New York: Continuum, 1995), 170.

28. Matthew 19:26.

29. 2 Corinthians 12:9.

30. Psalm 9:9.

Chapter 2: Let All Mortal Flesh Keep Silence

1. Catherine Clark Kroeger and Mary J. Evans, eds., "Luke," in *The IVP Women's Bible Commentary* (Downers Grove, IL: InterVarsity, 2002), 564.

2. R. C. Sproul, ed., *The Reformation Study Bible* (Lake Mary, FL: Ligonier, 2005), 1454, comment on Luke 1:19.

3. I. Howard Marshall, "Luke," in *The New Bible Commentary Revised* (Grand Rapids: Eerdmans, 1970), 890.

4. Walter L. Liefeld, "Luke," in *The Expositor's Bible Commentary* (Grand Rapids: Zondervan, 1984), 8:838.

5. Luke 1:62.

6. Walter C. Kaiser Jr. and Duane A. Garrett, eds., *NIV Archaeological Study Bible: An Illustrated Walk Through Biblical History and Culture* (Grand Rapids: Zondervan, 2005), 1665.

7. Numbers 6:24–26.

8. *Matthew Henry's Commentary on the Whole Bible* (Peabody, MA: Hendrickson, 1991), 5:470.

9. Ralph Gower, *The New Manners and Customs of Bible Times* (Chicago: Moody, 1987), 62.

10. Marshall, "Luke," 891.

11. Tremper Longman III, Mark L. Strauss, and Daniel Taylor, contributors, *The Expanded Bible: Explore the Depths of the Scriptures While You Read* (Nashville: Thomas Nelson, 2011), note on Luke 1:24.

12. Ross Saunders, *Outrageous Women, Outrageous God: Women in the First Two Generations of Christianity* (Alexandria, New South Wales, Australia: 1996), 68.

13. Saunders, *Outrageous Women, Outrageous God*, 68.

14. Kroeger and Evans, *IVP Women's Bible Commentary*, 564.

15. Christin Ditchfield, *The Three Wise Women: A Christmas Reflection* (Wheaton, IL: Crossway, 2005), 38.

16. Arlene Eisenberg, Heidi Eisenberg Murkoff, and Sandee Eisenberg Hathaway, *What to Expect When You're Expecting* (New York: Workman, 1984), 136.

17. Psalm 127:3, NLT.
18. Luke 1:6.
19. Ephesians 3:20.

Chapter 3: The Virgin Mother Kind

1. Walter L. Liefeld, "Luke," in *The Expositor's Bible Commentary* (Grand Rapids: Zondervan, 1984), 8:830.
2. Adam Hamilton, *The Journey: Walking the Road to Bethlehem* (Nashville: Abingdon, 2011), 15.
3. Frances Vander Velde, *Women of the Bible* (Grand Rapids: Kregel, 1985), 134.
4. John 1:46.
5. Ross Saunders, *Outrageous Women, Outrageous God: Women in the First Two Generations of Christianity* (Alexandria, New South Wales, Australia: 1996), 71.
6. Ralph Gower, *The New Manners and Customs of Bible Times* (Chicago: Moody, 1987), 65.
7. Howard F. Vos, *Nelson's New Illustrated Bible Manners and Customs: How the People of the Bible Really Lived* (Nashville: Thomas Nelson, 1999), 448.
8. Vos, *Illustrated Bible Manners and Customs,* 449.
9. Gower, *New Manners and Customs,* 155.
10. Gower, *New Manners and Customs,* 65.
11. I. Howard Marshall, "Luke," in *The New Bible Commentary Revised* (Grand Rapids: Eerdmans, 1970), 891.
12. Saunders, *Outrageous Women, Outrageous God,* 72.
13. Matthew 1:1.
14. Hamilton, *The Journey,* 21.
15. Isaiah 53:2.
16. Saunders, *Outrageous Women, Outrageous God,* 72.
17. Hamilton, *The Journey,* 22.
18. Hamilton, *The Journey,* 23.

19. Ruth 1:8.

20. 2 Samuel 14:17.

21. Luke 1:19.

22. Margaret E. Sangster, *The Women of the Bible: A Portrait Gallery* (New York: Christian Herald, 1911), 246.

23. Psalm 89:29.

24. Exodus 40:34.

25. Genesis 1:2.

26. Liefeld, "Luke," 8:832.

27. Genesis 18:14.

28. Christin Ditchfield, *The Three Wise Women: A Christmas Reflection* (Wheaton, IL: Crossway, 2005), 27.

29. Elizabeth George, *Women Who Loved God: A Devotional Walk with the Women of the Bible* (Eugene, OR: Harvest, 1999), September 24.

30. Catherine Clark Kroeger and Mary J. Evans, eds., "Luke," in *The IVP Women's Bible Commentary* (Downers Grove, IL: InterVarsity, 2002), 565.

31. Vander Velde, *Women of the Bible,* 138.

32. Isaiah 7:14.

Chapter 4: O Tidings of Comfort and Joy

1. Miriam Feinberg Vamosh, *Daily Life at the Time of Jesus* (Herzlia, Israel: Palphot, 2007), 52, 60.

2. Vamosh, *Daily Life,* 47.

3. Walter L. Liefeld, "Luke," in *The Expositor's Bible Commentary* (Grand Rapids: Zondervan, 1984), 8:834.

4. Adam Hamilton, *The Journey: Walking the Road to Bethlehem* (Nashville: Abingdon, 2011), 63.

5. Ross Saunders, *Outrageous Women, Outrageous God: Women in the First Two Generations of Christianity* (Alexandria, New South Wales, Australia: 1996), 74.

6. James M. Freeman, *Manners and Customs of the Bible* (New Kensington, PA: Whitaker, 1996), 330.

7. Catherine Clark Kroeger and Mary J. Evans, eds., "Luke," in *The IVP Women's Bible Commentary* (Downers Grove, IL: InterVarsity, 2002), 565.

8. Luke 1:36, CEV.

9. Luke 1:20, MOUNCE.

10. Hamilton, *The Journey,* 74.

11. Acts 2:1–4.

12. Luke 1:15, KNOX.

13. Judith A. Bauer, comp., *Advent and Christmas Wisdom from Henri J. M. Nouwen: Daily Scripture and Prayers Together with Nouwen's Own Words* (Liguori, MO: Liguori, 2004), 28.

14. Ephesians 2:4.

15. Lamentations 3:22.

16. John 3:30.

17. Galatians 5:22.

18. Ecclesia Bible Society, *The Voice Bible: Step into the Story of Scripture* (Nashville: Thomas Nelson, 2012), 1237.

19. Saunders, *Outrageous Women, Outrageous God,* 76.

20. Isaiah 58:6–8.

21. Matthew 5:3.

22. Matthew 5:5.

Chapter 5: With Heart and Soul and Voice

1. Psalm 71:6.

2. Miriam Feinberg Vamosh, *Women at the Time of the Bible* (Herzlia, Israel: Palphot, 2007), 46.

3. John 16:21.

4. Genesis 17:12–13.

5. James M. Freeman, *Manners and Customs of the Bible* (New Kensington, PA: Whitaker, 1996), 403.

6. "Jewish Names," Judaism 101, www.jewfaq.org/jnames .htm.

7. Catherine Clark Kroeger and Mary J. Evans, eds., "Luke," in *The IVP Women's Bible Commentary* (Downers Grove, IL: InterVarsity, 2002), 566.

8. Ross Saunders, *Outrageous Women, Outrageous God: Women in the First Two Generations of Christianity* (Alexandria, New South Wales, Australia: 1996), 69.

9. *Matthew Henry's Commentary on the Whole Bible* (Peabody, MA: Hendrickson, 1991), 5:470.

10. Freeman, *Manners and Customs,* 404.

11. Psalm 51:15.

12. Psalm 147:1.

13. Tremper Longman III, Mark L. Strauss, and Daniel Taylor, contributors, *The Expanded Bible: Explore the Depths of the Scriptures While You Read* (Nashville: Thomas Nelson, 2011), note on Luke 1:66.

14. Matthew 14:6–10.

15. Walter L. Liefeld, "Luke," in *The Expositor's Bible Commentary* (Grand Rapids: Zondervan, 1984), 8:839.

16. Liefeld, "Luke," 8:840.

17. Psalm 56:11.

18. Dorothy Kelley Patterson, ed., "Elizabeth: A Spiritual Mentor," in *The Woman's Study Bible* (Nashville: Thomas Nelson, 1995), 1687.

19. Matthew 11:11.

20. D. A. Carson, "Matthew," in *The Expositor's Bible Commentary* (Grand Rapids: Zondervan, 1984), 8:74.

21. Mike Rich, *The Nativity Story,* directed by Catherine Hardwicke (Burbank, CA: New Line Cinema, 2006).

22. Gien Karssen, *Her Name Is Woman* (Colorado Springs: NavPress, 1975), 1:132.

23. Albert Barnes, "Matthew," in *Notes on the New Testament,* ed. Robert Frew (Grand Rapids: Baker, 1998), 5.
24. Barnes, "Matthew," 5.
25. Barnes, "Matthew," 5.
26. R. C. Sproul, ed., *The Reformation Study Bible* (Lake Mary, FL: Ligonier, 2005), 1362, comment on Matthew 1:19.
27. Barnes, "Matthew," 5.
28. Walter C. Kaiser Jr. and Duane A. Garrett, eds., *NIV Archaeological Study Bible: An Illustrated Walk Through Biblical History and Culture* (Grand Rapids: Zondervan, 2005), 1560.
29. *Matthew Henry's Commentary,* 5:5.
30. Carson, "Matthew," 75.
31. Barnes, "Matthew," 6.
32. Arlene Eisenberg, Heidi Eisenberg Murkoff, and Sandee Eisenberg Hathaway, *What to Expect When You're Expecting* (New York: Workman, 1984), 148.
33. Luke 1:31.
34. Adam Hamilton, *The Journey: Walking the Road to Bethlehem* (Nashville: Abingdon, 2011), 47.
35. Luke 3:23.

Chapter 6: The Wondrous Gift Is Given

1. Micah 5:2.
2. Luke 1:37, ERV.
3. Psalm 50:10.
4. Isaiah 37:16.
5. Walter C. Kaiser Jr. and Duane A. Garrett, eds., *NIV Archaeological Study Bible: An Illustrated Walk Through Biblical History and Culture* (Grand Rapids: Zondervan, 2005), 1669.
6. Kaiser and Garrett, *NIV Archaeological Study Bible,* 1669.

7. I. Howard Marshall, "Luke," in *The New Bible Commentary Revised* (Grand Rapids: Eerdmans, 1970), 892.

8. Adam Hamilton, *The Journey: Walking the Road to Bethlehem* (Nashville: Abingdon, 2011), 30.

9. Hamilton, *The Journey,* 89.

10. Hamilton, *The Journey,* 90.

11. Hamilton, *The Journey,* 90.

12. Hamilton, *The Journey,* 90.

13. Anna Dintaman Landis, "Hiking the Nativity Trail from Nazareth to Bethlehem," Jesus Trail, December 18, 2010, http://jesustrail.com/blog/hiking-the-nativity-trail-from -nazareth-to-bethlehem.

14. John 1:14.

15. Exodus 13:21.

16. Albert Barnes, "Luke," in *Notes on the New Testament* (Grand Rapids: Baker, 1998), 17. See also Ezekiel 16:4.

17. Mary Eliza Rogers, *Domestic Life in Palestine* (Cincinnati: Poe and Hitchcock, 1865), 28.

18. Miriam Feinberg Vamosh, *Women at the Time of the Bible* (Herzlia, Israel: Palphot, 2007), 47.

19. John 20:16–18.

20. Mark 16:9.

21. *Matthew Henry's Commentary on the Whole Bible* (Peabody, MA: Hendrickson, 1991), 5:483.

22. Catherine Clark Kroeger and Mary J. Evans, eds., "Luke," in *The IVP Women's Bible Commentary* (Downers Grove, IL: InterVarsity, 2002), 566.

23. Barnes, "Luke," 17.

24. Barnes, "Luke," 18.

25. Virginia Stem Owens, *Daughters of Eve: Women of the Bible Speak to Women of Today* (Colorado Springs: NavPress, 1995), 30.

26. Kroeger and Evans, *IVP Women's Bible Commentary,* 566.

27. Luke 9:58.

28. *Matthew Henry's Commentary,* 5:483.

29. John 10:11.

30. Psalm 100:3.

31. R. C. Sproul, ed., *The Reformation Study Bible* (Lake Mary, FL: Ligonier, 2005), 1457, comment on Luke 2:8.

32. Sproul, *The Reformation Study Bible,* 1457, comment on Luke 2:8.

33. Kaiser and Garrett, *NIV Archaeological Study Bible,* 1669.

34. Proverbs 9:10.

35. Sproul, *The Reformation Study Bible,* 1457, comment on Luke 2:10.

36. *Matthew Henry's Commentary,* 5:484.

37. Job 38:7.

38. Psalm 71:23.

39. Isaiah 49:13, NLT.

40. *Matthew Henry's Commentary,* 5:484.

41. Barnes, "Luke," 19.

42. Job 19:25.

43. Luke 1:32.

44. Revelation 17:14.

45. Jude 1:24.

46. John 4:28–29.

47. Luke 2:11, GNT.

Chapter 7: And Our Eyes at Last Shall See Him

1. Adam Hamilton, *The Journey: Walking the Road to Bethlehem* (Nashville: Abingdon, 2011), 121.

2. Genesis 1:16.

3. *Matthew Henry's Commentary on the Whole Bible* (Peabody, MA: Hendrickson, 1991), 5:9.

4. Matthew 2:5–6.

5. Matthew 2:10, PHILLIPS.

6. Matthew 2:10, KJV.

7. Luke 1:32.

8. Genesis 17:13.

9. Bert Thompson, "Biblical Accuracy and Circumcision on the Eighth Day," Apologetics Press, www.apologeticspress.org /apcontent.aspx?category=13&article=1118.

10. Leviticus 12:2–4.

11. Leviticus 12:6–8.

12. Albert Barnes, "Luke," in *Notes on the New Testament* (Grand Rapids: Baker, 1998), 21.

13. Miriam Feinberg Vamosh, *Daily Life at the Time of Jesus* (Herzlia, Israel: Palphot, 2007), 23.

14. 2 Chronicles 16:9.

15. Romans 5:5.

16. *Matthew Henry's Commentary on the Whole Bible* (Peabody, MA: Hendrickson, 1991), 5:487.

17. Barnes, "Luke," 22.

18. John 1:17.

19. *Matthew Henry's Commentary,* 5:487.

20. Psalm 33:4, NIrV.

21. R. C. Sproul, ed., *The Reformation Study Bible* (Lake Mary, FL: Ligonier, 2005), 1458, comment on Luke 2:31.

22. Isaiah 42:6.

23. Elizabeth George, *Women Who Loved God: A Devotional Walk with the Women of the Bible* (Eugene, OR: Harvest, 1999), October 7.

24. John 19:34.

25. 1 Peter 5:7.

Chapter 8: Joy of Every Longing Heart

1. *Matthew Henry's Commentary on the Whole Bible* (Peabody, MA: Hendrickson, 1991), 5:489.
2. Philippians 3:12, PHILLIPS.
3. Exodus 15:20; Judges 4:4; 2 Kings 22:14; Nehemiah 6:14; Isaiah 8:3; Acts 21:8–9.
4. Joshua 19:24–31.
5. Rose Sallberg Kam, *Their Stories, Our Stories: Women of the Bible* (New York: Continuum, 1995), 168.
6. Claudia Gold, *Queen, Empress, Concubine: Fifty Women Rulers from the Queen of Sheba to Catherine the Great* (London: Quercus, 2009), 42, 56, 60.
7. Revelation 3:5.
8. Edith Deen, *All of the Women of the Bible* (New York: Harper and Row, 1955), 174.
9. Gien Karssen, *Her Name Is Woman* (Colorado Springs: NavPress, 1992), 1:150.
10. Ross Saunders, *Outrageous Women, Outrageous God: Women in the First Two Generations of Christianity* (Alexandria, New South Wales, Australia: 1996), 31.
11. Miriam Feinberg Vamosh, *Women at the Time of the Bible* (Herzlia, Israel: Palphot, 2007), 39.
12. 1 Timothy 5:5.
13. Walter C. Kaiser Jr. and Duane A. Garrett, eds., *NIV Archaeological Study Bible: An Illustrated Walk Through Biblical History and Culture* (Grand Rapids: Zondervan, 2005), 1648.
14. Ann Spangler and Jean E. Syswerda, *Women of the Bible: A One-Year Devotional Study of Women in Scripture* (Grand Rapids: Zondervan, 1999), 311.
15. Frances Vander Velde, *Women of the Bible* (Grand Rapids: Kregel, 1985), 161.

16. Joy Jacobs, *They Were Women Like Me: Women of the New Testament in Devotions for Today* (Camp Hill, PA: Christian Publications, 1993), 40.

17. Edith Deen, *Wisdom from Women in the Bible* (New York: HarperCollins, 2003), 137.

18. Psalm 27:4.

19. Albert Barnes, "Luke," in *Notes on the New Testament* (Grand Rapids: Baker, 1998), 24.

20. Scott Hagan, *They Walked with the Savior: Twenty Ordinary People in the Gospels Who Had Extraordinary Encounters with God* (Lake Mary, FL: Charisma, 2002), 164.

21. 1 Corinthians 7:34.

22. *Matthew Henry's Commentary,* 5:489.

23. Deen, *All of the Women,* 172.

24. Vander Velde, *Women of the Bible,* 133.

25. *Matthew Henry's Commentary,* 5:489.

26. Karssen, *Her Name Is Woman,* 152.

27. 2 Timothy 4:8.

28. Saunders, *Outrageous Women, Outrageous God,* 31.

29. Kam, *Their Stories, Our Stories,* 170.

30. Psalm 68:11.

31. Hebrews 2:17.

32. *Matthew Henry's Commentary,* 5:490.

Study Guide

1. R. C. Sproul, ed., *The Reformation Study Bible* (Lake Mary, FL: Ligonier, 2005), 1454, comment on Luke 1:19.

2. Jeremiah 32:17.

3. Carolyn Custis James, *Lost Women of the Bible: Finding Strength and Significance Through Their Stories* (Grand Rapids: Zondervan, 2005), 166.

4. Carolyn Nabors Baker, *Caught in a Higher Love: Inspiring Stories of Women in the Bible* (Nashville: Broadman and Holman, 1998), 7.

5. D. A. Carson, "Matthew," in *The Expositor's Bible Commentary* (Grand Rapids: Zondervan, 1984), 8:81.

6. 1 Samuel 2:3.

7. Scott Hagan, *They Walked with the Savior: Twenty Ordinary People in the Gospels Who Had Extraordinary Encounters with God* (Lake Mary, FL: Charisma, 2002), 165.

Additional Bible Versions

American Standard Version (ASV). Amplified Bible (AMP). Copyright © 1954, 1958, 1962, 1964, 1965, 1987 by The Lockman Foundation. Used by permission. Common English Bible (CEB). Copyright © 2011 by Common English Bible. Complete Jewish Bible (CJB). Copyright © 1998 by David H. Stern. All rights reserved. Contemporary English Version (CEV). Copyright © 1991, 1992, 1995 by American Bible Society. Used by permission. Douay-Rheims 1899 American Edition (DRA). Easy-to-Read Version (ERV). Copyright © 2006 World Bible Translation Center. English Standard Version (ESV), copyright © 2001 by Crossway Bibles, a division of Good News Publishers. Used by permission. All rights reserved. Expanded Bible (EXB). Copyright © 2011 by Thomas Nelson, Inc. Used by permission. All rights reserved. Geneva Bible (GNV), 1599 edition. Published by Tolle Lege Press. All rights reserved. God's Word (GOD'S WORD), a copyrighted work of God's Word to the Nations Bible Society. Quotations are used by permission. Copyright 1995 by God's Word to the Nations. All rights reserved. Good News Translation—Second Edition (GNT). Copyright © 1992 by American Bible Society. Used by permission. Holman Christian Standard Bible® (HCSB). Copyright © 1999, 2000, 2002, 2003, 2009 by Holman Bible Publishers. Used by permission. Holman Christian Standard Bible®, Holman CSB®, and HCSB® are federally registered trademarks of Holman Bible Publishers. J. B. Phillips (PHILLIPS), The New Testament in Modern English, Revised Edition © 1972 by J. B. Phillips. Copyright renewed © 1986, 1988 by Vera M. Phillips. King James Version (KJV). Knox Translation of the Bible (KNOX) by Monsignor Ronald Knox. Copyright © 2012 by Westminster Diocese. Lexham English Bible (LEB). Copyright 2012 by Logos Bible Software. Lexham is a registered trademark of Logos Bible Software. The Message (MSG) by Eugene H. Peterson. Copyright © 1993, 1994, 1995, 1996, 2000, 2001, 2002. Used by permission of NavPress Publishing Group. All rights reserved. Mounce Reverse-Interlinear™ New Testament (MOUNCE). Copyright © 2011 by Robert H. Mounce and William D. Mounce. Used by permission. All rights reserved worldwide. New American Standard Bible® (NASB). © Copyright The Lockman Foundation 1960, 1962, 1963, 1968, 1971, 1972, 1973, 1975, 1977, 1995. Used by permission. (www.Lockman.org). New Century Version® (NCV). Copyright © 1987, 1988, 1991, 2005 by Thomas Nelson Inc. Used by permission. All rights reserved. New English Translation (NET), NET Bible®, copyright © 1996-2006 by Biblical Studies Press, LLC, www.bible.org. Used by permission. All rights reserved. New International Reader's Version® (NIrV). NIV®. Copyright © 1995, 1996, 1998 by Biblica Inc.™ Used by permission of Zondervan. All rights reserved worldwide. www.zondervan.com. New King James Version® (NKJV). Copyright © 1982 by Thomas Nelson Inc. Used by permission. All rights reserved. Holy Bible, New Life Version (NLV). Copyright 1969, 1976, 1978, 1983, 1986, 1992, 1997,

Heartfelt Thanks

The Women of Christmas began as an online Bible study during the Advent season. What a blessing it's been to gather all those words and many more between the covers of this book.

The thousands of sisters and brothers in Christ who faithfully read my Bible study blog are dear to me. I'm especially grateful for those readers who respond by posting comments that come from the deepest recesses of their hearts.

You have met some of those kind souls among these pages: Miriam, Sherry, Marbara, Steph, Stacy, Tina, Kirra, Liz, Nicole, Susan, Elizabeth, Cathy, Shelly, Elisabeth, Ann, Chari, Christina, Michele, Brenda, Alina, Lisa, Candy, Phyllis, Tracy, Shari, Tosin, Rhetta, Karen, Robin. Thank you, sisters, for allowing me the privilege of sharing your words.

To follow my weekly Bible study blog, kindly visit www.LizCurtisHiggs.com/blog/ and subscribe to receive it in your e-mail inbox.

A big hug to my editorial team, whose abundant patience and gentle direction make the editing process *almost* painless: Laura Barker, Carol Bartley, Sara Fortenberry, Rebecca Price, Bill Higgs, Helen Macdonald, Rose Decaen, and Matthew

Higgs. Special thanks to Allison O'Hara at WaterBrook Multnomah, whose initial enthusiasm for this project helped put things in motion.

Finally, to the whole team at Women of Faith, especially my dear speaking sisters: thank you for welcoming me into your fold, and bless you for all you do to celebrate Jesus. What *joy* to share the stories of Elizabeth and Mary for our 2013 tour, Believe God Can Do Anything!

A Novel Approach to Bible Study

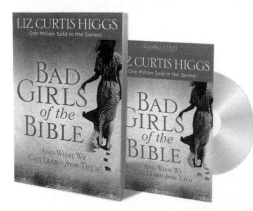

With one million copies sold, *Bad Girls of the Bible* breathes new life into the ancient stories about ten of the most infamous—and intriguing—women in history, from Eve to Jezebel. An eye-opening, life-changing study.

Liz Curtis Higgs dishes out meat and milk, substance and style, in a highly readable, always entertaining, and deeply personal journey through the book of Ruth.

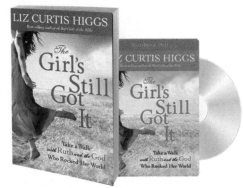

Companion DVDs work perfectly for Bible studies and small groups.

To learn more, visit www.waterbrookmultnomah.com.

WATERBROOK
PRESS

Three women named MARY,
one SAVIOR *called* JESUS.

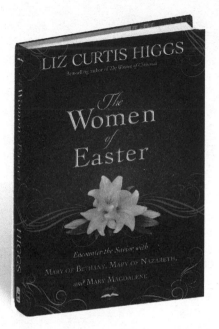

Prepare for a life-changing encounter with Jesus through the eyes of three women who know Him—Mary of Bethany, Mary of Nazareth, and Mary Magdalene.

Read a sample at WaterBrookMultnomah.com.
Available in bookstores January 2017!